Hymns from the Four Winds

JUNGREA CHUNG

A COLLECTION OF
ASIAN AMERICAN HYMNS

Hymns from the Four Winds

SUPPLEMENTAL WORSHIP RESOURCES 13

ABINGDON PRESS
Nashville

HYMNS FROM THE FOUR WINDS

ISBN 0-687-18126-7

MANUFACTURED BY THE PARTHENON PRESS AT
NASHVILLE, TENNESSEE, UNITED STATES OF AMERICA

9426732

Acknowledgments

Hymns from the Four Winds is the product of many dedicated writers, poets, translators, composers, and arrangers, and others from United Methodist and ecumenical circles who have directly or indirectly participated in this project during the last two years.

We are grateful to the Reverend Jonah Chang, whose vision and enthusiasm have brought this project to reality; to Dr. Richard Eslinger, whose insight, criticism, and supervision have upgraded the quality of these hymns; to Mrs. Dorothy Turner-Lacy, Mrs. JoAnn Eslinger, and the Ethnic Minority Local Church staff, for their generous support and interest; to Dr. Hoyt Hickman and other staff in the Section on Worship, Board of Discipleship, for their support and encouragement.

A sincere gratitude is extended to the members of the editorial committee, whose names appear below, for their talents, dedication, and cooperation, without which this hymnbook would not have been completed. We are also indebted to Miss Esther Rice and Mrs. Elise Shoemaker who have taken pains to paraphrase, versify, and improve a large number of hymns. Special thanks to Elise, who prepared the topical index and willingly undertook the responsibility from the second proof to its publication after the editor left the country. An acknowledgment is made here to the Reverend Frank Ohtomo, who has kindly prepared the biblical references. I am grateful to my children for their clerical assistance, and most of all to my wife, Hui-chin, who has been indispensable throughout the entire project, as secretary and critic, helping me prepare the final draft and all the indexes. Without her dedication and patient support, I could not have completed the editorial work.

Acknowledgment is made here to all individuals who have granted permission for use of their texts and music, especially to the Hymn Committee of the United Church of Christ in Japan and the Ecumenical Committee of New Hymns in Korea, for their kind permission to translate and reprint their copyrighted hymns; to the Chinese Christian Literature Council, Hong Kong, for their permission to reprint some of their English versions of selections from *Hymns of Universal Praise;* and to the Christian Conference of Asia, for the use of some of the materials in their *Hymnal Supplement I,* which I helped compile. Every effort has been made to secure permission for publication; if acknowledgment of copyright is not given, we offer our sincere apologies and add the assurance that we will do our utmost to correct this in future editions.

Preface

Hymns from the Four Winds is a collection of music and texts drawn largely from Asian and Asian American sources. Much of the material is newly written or recently recovered and adapted. One result of this editorial decision to emphasize distinctly Asian traditions is that *Hymns from the Four Winds* is more truly indigenous to the various Asian churches represented than many hymnals now in use by those communities. Through this process of recovery and new composition by Asian and Asian American musicians, this hymnal offers enrichment to the worship of the entire ecumenical church.

The editorial committee for *Hymns from the Four Winds* consists of:
> I-to Loh, editor
> Keh-ming Liu, Chinese
> Lois F. Bello, Filipino
> Jonathan Fujita, Japanese
> T. Tom Lee, Korean
> Thomas Tai, Taiwanese
> Richard Eslinger was the liaison
> to the project from
> the Section on Worship.

The Section on Worship of the Board of Discipleship is the sponsor of this Asian American hymnal, which is the thirteenth publication in its Supplemental Worship Resources (SWR) series. The National Federation of Asian American United Methodists provided invaluable assistance and support. Jonah Chang is the Executive Director of the National Federation. Elise Shoemaker provided assistance in final editing and manuscript preparation.

Members of the Section on Worship (1981–84) include:
> Stan DePano, Chairperson
> George W. Watson
> J. Sue Kana
> George W. Bashore
> Donald Bueg
> D. S. Dharmapalan
> Melissa Lynn Ives
> Merwin Kurtz
> Cindy K. Locklear

Mary Penn
Luis Sotomayor
Sharon Spieth
Carole Cotton-Winn

Section on Worship staff include Ezra Earl Jones, General Secretary; Noé Gonzales, Associate General Secretary; Hoyt Hickman, Assistant General Secretary; Richard Eslinger, Barbara García and Judy Loehr.

The United Methodist Publishing House Staff include John E. Procter, President and Publisher; Ronald P. Patterson, Book Editor; Robert J. Hill, Managing Editor; Linda Bryant and Mada Johnston.

Foreword

After so many continually tragic war experiences in Asia, the 1970s saw new hope of peace and prosperity. However, the United States, being located on the eastern end of the Pacific Ocean, again is getting more and more deeply involved with the other side of the "basin." Asians in exodus gave threatening impressions of refugees, unending waves of immigration, new religions and economic invasions, counteracting any appreciation of culture or expression of faith and Christian living that the Asian Christians brought to the worshiping community here on the American scene.

At the core of Christian worship is music. Asians, being unused to music as an expression of worship, hesitated in exploring this aspect of the Christian faith. Their acceptance of music evolved through three stages. In the first stage, Asian Christians learned to appreciate the music that communicated the messages of salvation and newness of life. During this stage, the sharing was strictly one way—from Euro-American to Asian hymnals. The tunes sounded entirely foreign, and the messages appeared primitive to Asians. Next came the stage of imitation and adaptation. During this stage Asians learned to atune themselves to the Christian West. Many have learned hymnology and musician-ship thoroughly, their knowledge exceeding that of their Greco-Roman-European counterparts. But now, the end of twentieth century ushers in the stage of liberated Asians who have begun to bear fruits of their cultural and confessional roots. By liberated Asians, I mean the artists who dare to test the vast numbers of vehicles that carry the breadth of Christian life and the depth of the Christian message to human hearts everywhere. In order to make Christian witness worldwide, the vehicles developed by Euro-Americans are no longer adequate or capable. To let all tongues sing the songs of salvation is to set free forms and tunes thought to be unfit and suppressed by the Christian West, to be reappreciated and to be shared. This is a glorious period in which we Christians live to sing, to praise, and to confess in tunes that are familiar to or representative of the majority of the world population. In presenting the Asian American hymn, I feel like shouting out, "Now let us sing as the world is used to singing to the Creator and Redeemer!"

The task of translation has been very difficult because we Asian Americans are from diverse cultures and languages. However, since we now live on the North American continent, the medium of English is beneficial not only for Asian Americans but also for the English-speaking world. When you sing these hymns please remember how unfamiliar it was for the non–Euro-Americans to sing and appreciate the "Christian hymns" that were brought by the missionaries to many Asian countries. The difference this time is that those who are familiar with the kinds of tunes included in this hymn book are definitely more in number than the population in the so-called Christian West.

Gratitude is owed to the Board of Discipleship for affirming the need of Asian

Americans and channeling the Ethnic Minority Local Church funds for this hymnbook project; also we should like to acknowledge The United Methodist Church as a whole for making the strengthening of Ethnic Minority Local Church a missional priority. Confidence in digging into their roots and expressing their heritage as well as their joy and praise as Christians is the basic ingredient to strengthening the Asian American local church. Besides their soul-searching, the Asian Americans have been the ones to demonstrate their spirit and enthusiasm of church expansion in the past decade. For the insight and vision for this Asian American hymnbook project, the Board of Directors of the National Federation needs to be commended for their decision in 1979 to allow the formation of an editorial committee and to present a project proposal to the United Methodist General Conference in 1980. This became the instrument of Christian witness through music. The National Federation is a Christian body in which twelve caucuses come under the umbrella of unity and cooperation. The twelve "tribes" at the present time are five jurisdictional/geographical and six ethnic caucuses and one women's caucus of United Methodist Asian Americans.

Even though the torch of the project was carried by The United Methodist Church, it was nevertheless every bit ecumenical. There were many contributors, critics, supporters, and interpreters from many Protestant denominations and the Roman Catholic community.

My special thanks go to the editorial committee. The contributive backbone of this hymnbook is formed by the diligent members of the editorial committee, led by the most able and dedicated editor, I-to Loh. Loh was a professor of church music at Tainan Theological College and was active in the Asian scene before coming to the University of California at Los Angeles for his Ph.D. degree. He is well known in the Asian Christian community through his participation in the Christian Conference of Asia and through his editorship of *The New Songs of Asian Cities,* 1972. He is not only a gifted artist who composes, sings, criticizes, and educates, but also a talented administrator who has collected, sorted, and arranged all he has into an orderly piece of collective work. Words are not enough to express my gratitude and appreciation to I-to Loh for this monument to the global community of Christians, especially around the Pacific Basin.

In conclusion, the suffering and struggling Christians of Asia come to mind. Many Christian leaders are imprisoned because they side with the poor, powerless, and oppressed. While singing these Asian American hymns, we long for the day when both oppressors and oppressed may be set free. As the writer of the song "Lamentation of the Wanderer" expresses well, "Slaves in Egypt were set free, even after four hundred years; we have all been wand'ring for a long time, hoping freedom will come some day." Together we hope that freedom will come to our colleagues on the other side of the Pacific. Only then will freedom come to us on both sides of the basin.

Jonah Chang
Executive Director

National Federation of
Asian American United
Methodists

Editor's Introduction

The United States consists of peoples from all over the world who have brought diversified cultures, resources, and talents that have contributed to the formation and nourishment of this unique country. Indeed, all people here, including the native Americans, are immigrants or descendants of immigrants. Like the early pilgrim fathers searching for freedom, opportunity, and equality, Asian Americans have also come. They have introduced aspects of Asian cultures, contributing to this melting pot of world cultures. We have all gathered "from the four winds" (Matthew 24:31; Mark 13:27), and are in the process of uniting the family of God; we are beginning to sing new songs to the Lord.

The Asian American hymnbook project was launched in late 1979 with the following purposes:

1. To preserve the rich Asian cultural heritages among the new and old immigrants.
2. To encourage respect and self-awareness of the individual culture.
3. To help ministers, seminarians, and lay persons understand and appreciate Asian Christian heritages.
4. To stimulate composition and performance of new Asian American hymns.
5. To share diversified Christian experiences and to improve international communication and fellowship.
6. To explore new possibilities for minority group contributions to ecumenical families.

In order to accomplish such goals, letters were sent out to Asian American communities, soliciting their input and contributions, and an Asian American Hymnbook Editorial Committee was formed with representatives from five major ethnic groups who are members of the National Federation of Asian American United Methodists: Chinese, Filipino, Japanese, Korean, and Taiwanese. A director/editor was appointed, and each ethnic group organized its individual subcommittees to carry out plans for promotion, collection, improvement, and recommendation of new hymns. From the beginning the major obstacle in this project was that Asian American hymns as such were almost nonexistent. In the first place, there are few Asian American poets and composers, particularly Christian ones, interested in hymn writing. Second, since hymn writing is a specialized field of composition, we found few with such technical expertise. Frustrated by the lack of suitable material, some of us could not help searching our respective homelands for new and old hymns. All those factors account for the number of translations and reprints from certain groups. Because a balance of contributions from each ethnic group was sought, no attempt was made to address all the usual contents of a conventional hymnal. The works that have been composed or translated especially for this project, or those which are being published for the first time, are identified by a small circle (°). To help users of this book gain insight and understanding of Asian American hymns, we have provided the following explanations.

I. Text and Translation

Except for the Filipino hymns and a few others, which were of Western origin, the majority of hymns in this collection are translations. It is common knowledge that cultural expressions and nuances are very difficult to translate into other languages. Hymn translation demands faithfulness to the original text, clarity of expression, and poetic beauty. Such demands are difficult to meet when few of us are well equipped with poetic talents. In addition to the linguistic handicaps, we had to overcome three problems: (1) strict metrical structure and rhyming scheme, (2) sex-exclusive language, and (3) archaic language. For metrical structures, we frequently found it necessary to alter the meter, adding or omitting extra syllables to make the meaning clear, and in some cases changing the musical rhythms to accommodate the text. Thus irregularity in meter is unavoidable, and rhyming, which is so important in hymns, subsequently had to be sacrificed for the sake of clarity. We regret to say that this also led us to omit a metrical index. We have followed the general guidelines for sex-inclusive language and have made every effort to use nouns and pronouns that refer to people of both sexes. "Father" and "he" referring to God have also been replaced, when possible, by other words; but direct quotations from the Bible have been retained. We also preferred familiar English over archaic language. Some familiar texts that do not conform to the above principles, or texts by authors who objected to our changes, have not been altered, for fear of impairing the beauty and integrity of the original texts. Realizing all the limitations and complexities of compiling this hymnal, we should appreciate comments and suggestions for revision in future editions.

II. Musical Styles

The music in this collection represents the following styles:
1. Traditional melodies from the respective cultures with or without foreign influences.
2. Imitations of Western gospel song styles as taught by early missionaries.
3. Adaptations from folk and/or newly created melodies with Western harmony.
4. Native or original melodies with harmonic idioms different from those of the West.
5. Contemporary Western musical styles.
6. Combination of more than one style in a single hymn.

Many east Asian traditional melodies are in pentatonic scales, with or without the interval of a semitone and are without harmony. With the introduction of Christianity, gospel songs and harmony were introduced to Asian soil; and they have been accepted and imitated. Many Asian churches are still in this early stage of imitation, but some have begun to adapt folk melodies or to compose new ones in their traditional idioms, and traditional Western four-part harmony was added. Some of these experiments in Asia have found minor success; others have disrupted their native music, for it is difficult to find a common ground in which different musical systems can be combined. Today, some serious Asian church music composers are deeply concerned with the dilemma of communicating their Christian faith to their own people in a meaningful, contemporary musical language that will at the same time maintain the integrity of their own traditions.

In this Asian American setting, we should be well acquainted not only with the development in our native lands, but also the contemporary western musical idioms. We would like to point out, however, that a major difference among some Asian musics is their monophonic nature, i.e., melody without harmony; their music generally emphasizes the beauty in melody, rhythm, and color or timbre. This is why so many hymns are to be sung in unison. Although harmony is foreign to some of them, Asian music can be effectively contextualized for our modern use, with proper understanding of their musical styles, and with skillful handling of multipart techniques without destroying their integrity and beauty. Performers will see the process of acculturation and will feel some of the struggles for contextualization in some of the hymns here. We would like to emphasize that the *Hymns from the Four Winds* is not a mature product; it is rather a record of the Asian American Christians' pilgrimage and spiritual growth. This pilgrimage has brought the gospel back to the "mother church" with their own interpretations—some with the same musical language first taught by the missionaries; others with the new languages that have been developed in the native or contemporary styles. Theologically speaking, some hymns show evangelical, pietistic, and devotional characteristics; others exhibit deep concern for social justice and the church's involvement in contemporary issues. This hymnbook, therefore, is the "firstfruits" of the newest immigrants; it represents not only their search for their Asian roots but also their contributions to this newly adopted country. These writers and composers have just sowed their seeds, which await further cultivation, nourishment, and eventual harvest.

III. Performance Suggestions

Sixty-one percent of the texts in this collection are newly written or translated, and over forty-five percent of the music is newly composed, adapted, or arranged, which means that the hymns may not be familiar to most congregations. It may sound strange, but Asian Americans who feel at home with Western hymns and gospel songs may find hymns written in Asian styles foreign to them. Western-oriented musicians may also find some of the music "weird" or "exotic." Those who are attracted by these musics and feel like adding "harmony" to them should do so *only* within the framework of that particular style. As a general practice, we would like to offer the following performance suggestions. Specific instructions for particular pieces can be found under some of the hymns.

1. Prepare and practice the hymn with the choir and congregation ahead of time, so that they can participate with reasonable confidence.
2. When the hymn is not familiar to the congregation, it is advisable to play the whole hymn through once; otherwise, a short introduction, as indicated by ⌐ ¬ . . . ⌐ ¬ will suffice.
3. The metronome mark (♩ = c.80) is but a suggested tempo; it may be faster or slower according to size or preference of the group, or familiarity with the hymn.
4. When the music appears to be difficult, play only the melody with the doubling in the octave. An experienced accompanist may be able to simplify or improvise the

accompaniment within the appropriate style after the congregation feels comfortable in singing the hymn.

5. The choir may play an important role in introducing new hymns by a "lining out" technique,—i.e., the congregation repeating after the choir line by line.

6. Try to create variety with unison by
   a) responsorial singing: alternating solo (male/female) with chorus (M/F or mixed)
   b) antiphonal singing: sectional alternation between groups
   c) change of registration and a capella
   d) change of tempo
   e) alternating between singing and reciting

7. It is customary for songs of the Indian subcontinent to be repeated within each section, but if they seem "too long," the repetition signs, except the refrain for the last stanza, may be ignored.

8. Where appropriate, ethnic instruments may be employed to double the melody or to accompany the piece. Some people find the use of organ or piano with ethnic instruments acceptable; others feel awkward about such combinations. In any case, they should be handled with extreme care. It may take some time to get used to these accompaniments. We therefore would leave this matter to your own discretion. The following numbered symbols (#), as indicated under some hymns, provide general suggestions for use of particular instruments appropriate to the respective cultures; some of the instruments may be substituted for or combined with other instruments as necessary.

#1 Wind instrument (ti-tsŭ, taekeum, ryūteki, or flute)
#2 Double reed instrument (hichiriki, or oboe)
#3 Bowed lute (erh-hu, haekeum, kokyū, or violin)
#4 Plucked lute (ṕ i-ṕ a, biwa, or shamisen)
#5 Zither (cheng, kayakeum, koto)
#6 Drum (tabla, mridangam, ku changko, taiko)

Contents

1

Praise and Adoration

Behold the Man

MABUNE

Kō Yūki, 1923
Trans. by Vern Rossman

Seigi Abe, 1930

(♩ = c. 96)

1. In a low - ly man - ger born, Hum - ble life be - gun in scorn.
2. Vis - it - ing for - got - ten ones, Draw - ing them to God a - gain,
3. Came to earth for you and me, Gave his life up - on the tree,

In a work - shop Je - sus grew, Work - man's life he knew.
Giv - ing of him - self in love God's own love to prove.
See in him God's love re - vealed; By his suf - f'rings healed.

Knew the suf - f'ring of the weak, Knew the long - ing of the meek,
Sin - ners glad - ly heard his call, Pub - li - cans be - fore him fall
Lives a - gain in glo - ry bright, Lives a - gain in pow'r and might,

Knew the poor as but they can, This is he, Be - hold the man!
And in him new life be - gan, This is he, Be - hold the man!
Now we know sal - va - tion's plan, God in Christ has lived as man.

Music and words used by permission of the Japanese Hymnal Committee.

Matthew 8:20; John 19:5

Japanese

JESUS CHRIST

2 Give Us, O God, the Grace to See

ROGER KRONMANN

JORDAN

JORDON CHO-TUNG TANG, 1970

1. Give us, O God, the grace to see Your smile with-in the morn-ing light; Your sig - na - ture up - on the sea; Your shad - ow in the black - est night.
2. Give us, O God, the grace to hear Your Word when mar - ble turns to clay; Your voice when thun - der clouds ap - pear; Your an - swer when the moun - tains sway.
3. Give us, O God, the grace to feel Your breath up - on the winds of change; Your kiss in sac - ra - ments that heal; Your hand in what the years ar - range.
4. Give us, O God, the grace to be Con-vinced when mir - a - cles are rare; Your truth when stars turn eb - o - ny; Your saints till earth has no de - spair. A - men.

Music from *Hymns of Universal Praise*, revised edition. Copyright © 1977 by the Chinese Christian Literature Council Ltd., Hong Kong.

Mark 7:33-34, 10:46-52

THE GOODNESS AND PROVIDENCE OF GOD

Chinese

God Created Heaven and Earth

TŌA-SĪA

Traditional
Trans. by Boris and Clare Anderson, °rev., 1981

Pin-po° melody
Harm. by I-to Loh, 1963, °rev., 1982

1. God cre - a - ted heav'n and earth, All things per - fect brought to birth; God's great pow'r made dark and light Earth re -volv -ing day and night.
2. Let us praise God's mer - cy great, All our needs that love a - wait; God, who fash - ions all that lives, To each one a bless - ing gives.
3. God is One, will ev - er be: I - dols are mere van - i - ty; Hand - made gods of wood and clay, Can - not help us when we pray.
4. But God's grace be - yond com - pare Saves us all from death's de - spair; So earth's crea - tures small and great, Give thanks for that bless - ed state.

Psalm 148

Taiwanese

GOD'S CREATION

4   God of Concrete, God of Steel

HUNAN

RICHARD G. JONES, 1968

Chinese folksong
Arr. by W. H. WONG, 1977

1. God of concrete, God of steel, God of piston and of wheel, God of pylon, and of steam, God of girder and of beam, God of atom, God of mine, All the world of pow'r is thine.

2. Lord of cable, Lord of rail, Lord of motor-way and mail, Lord of rocket, Lord of flight, Lord of soaring satellite, Lord of lightning's livid line, All the world of speed is thine.

3. Lord of science, Lord of art, God of map and graph and chart, Lord of physics and research, Word of Bible, Faith of church, Lord of sequence and design, All the world of truth is thine.

4. God whose glory fills the earth, Gave the universe its birth, Loosed the Christ with Easter's might, Saves the world from evil's blight, Claims mankind by grace divine, All the world of love is thine.

GOD'S CREATION

Chinese

God the Lord in Love and Might 5

TAMSUI

Traditional
Trans. by BORIS and CLARE ANDERSON, °rev., 1981

Pin-po° melody
Harm. by I-TO LOH, 1963, °rev., 1982

Unison (♩ = c. 92)

1. God, the Lord in love and might Shaped cre - a - tion
2. Sun that fills the sky with light, Moon and stars that
3. Ev - 'ry grain which earth doth yield, Flow'r and fruit and
4. Birds that fly a - bove our head, By the hands of
5. Peo - ple too in ev - 'ry land, Live by God's all
6. One is God, the Lord a - lone, I - dols are but

in - fi - nite; So that to One
shine by night, Hill and val - ley
grass - y field, Fish that swim in
God are fed; In - sects crawl - ing
boun - teous hand; God a - lone their
wood and stone; God a - lone to

Name we raise Songs of won - der and of praise.
high and low, God's great pow'r and glo - ry show.
stream and sea, God made each so per - fect - ly.
at our feet, Share God's prov-i - dence com - plete.
need pro - vides and their way in all things guides.
us can be Life that flows e - ter - nal - ly.

Harm. copyright © 1983 by I-to Loh.
Trans. copyright © 1983 by Boris and Clare Anderson.

Psalm 24

Taiwanese

GOD'S CREATION

6 God, We Praise You for This Lord's Day

P'U-T'O

Tzu-chen Chao, 1931
Trans. by Frank W. Price, 1953

Buddhist Chant
Harm. by Bliss Wiant, 1934

(♩ = c. 88)

1. God, we praise you for this Lord's day, Praise your good - ness
2. Af - ter toil - ing through the long week, Now we come to
3. Some - times we bear pain and sor - row, Some - times dark - ness
4. Some - times we find peace and glad - ness, Calm and hope in
5. Here we come our lives to of - fer, Hearts and minds we

now and al - way. By your grace we all do live;
hear your voice speak. In your house may all be blessed,
hides the mor - row, Lov - ing, Lord God, leave us not
joy or sad - ness; On our way you shed your light,
hum - bly prof - fer. Dear Lord, hear us while we pray,

In your mer - cy you for - give.
Here may all find strength and rest.
When sore trou - ble is our lot.
Love us ev - er, day and night.
And re - ceive us now for aye. A - men.

Psalm 118:24

THE GOODNESS AND PROVIDENCE OF GOD

Chinese

Great Are Your Mercies, Heavenly Father 7

SONG OF THE HOE

Tzu-chen Chao, 1981
Trans. by Frank W. Price, 1953

Chinese folksong
Harm. W. H. Wong, 1977

(♩ = c. 100)

1. Great are your mer - cies, Heaven - ly Fa - ther, Food and
2. Be not so anx - ious, sis - ters, broth - ers, What you
3. Birds of the air fly here and yon - der, Lil - ies
4. Could Sol - o - mon in all his glo - ry Match these

rai - ment you do still be - stow. Let me praise
dai - ly eat and what you wear. For our God
bloom, ar - rayed by na - ture thus; They sow not,
bril - liant birds and love - ly flowers? Sis - ters, broth - ers,

you al - ways, Serve you all my days. You the
sees and knows All our wants and woes. Hum - bly
and reap not, Nei - ther do they spin. Our Pro -
do not fret; God's love fails not yet. This world

spring wind, I the grass; On me blow!
let us work and trust God's great care.
vid - er cares for them. More for us!
God made is your home, Yours and ours.

Matthew 6:25-34

Chinese

THE GOODNESS AND PROVIDENCE OF GOD

8

Grandeur of God

DEV TUMA MAV

E. Walter Marasinghe
Trans. by James Minchin, 1980

E. Walter Marasinghe, 1980

(♩ = c. 88)

1. Full of won-drous beau - ty are God's cre - a - tive ways;
2. Moun-tains raise their spires to the vault of the sky,
3. Fierce are the beasts who must kill for their food—
4. Sun by day gives warmth, brings each new bud to flow'r;
5. I can frame no words which will match the an - gel's psalms.

Come now, my friends, His Spir - it sends Joy to our lips to pro-
Riv - ers de-scend Slopes with-out end; Here for-ests thrive as their
Lions' warn-ing growl, Wolves' cru - el howl; Play-ful the deer and young
Moon's lus-trous light Res - cues the night; Who but the Lord can or -
Heav - en and earth Tell of God's worth. All we can do is to

claim His praise. Maj - es - ty be-longs To His name al-ways.
trees push up high; There the des - ert spreads, Sand dunes parched and dry.
ele - phants' mood; God a - lone can call All that He makes good.
dain in His pow'r Worlds both great and small, Each to have its hour?
rest in God's arms Cap-tured by His name, Love, and Love's sweet charms.

Psalm 148

Performance suggestions: See #1 on page xii. No harmony to be added.
GOD'S CREATION

Sri Lankan

9

° Your Spirit in All Majesty

°APPLEGATE

Tetsuro P. Sano, 1973
Alt. by Elise Shoemaker, 1981

Tetsuro P. Sano, 1973
Harm. by Yuri L. Torigoe
Alt., AAH, 1981

Majestic (♩ = c. 88)

1. The rock - y peaks of moun-tains stand - ing tall, and qui - et
2. The soar - ing gran - ite cliff, El Cap - i - tan, Grand Can-yon's
3. As in all na - ture you have shown your love, in skies a -
4. We raise our thanks to you Al - might - y God, for grace you

GOD'S CREATION

Japanese

pas - tures at riv - er's side; The sculp-tured cliffs and broad white
rug - ged an - cient face; In Zi - on's red - rock tow - 'ring
bove, on earth be - low; We al - so know your grace in
give to make us free, O Lord, we wor - ship you in

sand - y shores and waves that roll in un - ceas - ing tide — In cre - a - tion
mon - u ments, and Te - ton's peak in mist - y haze — Na - ture shows your
all our days, through joy and pain you help us grow. You, who of - fer
Je - sus Christ, your Spir - it in all maj - es - ty. Lead us for - ward

clear - ly show God's great pow'r re - vealed and known. Both des - ert
hand - i - works, pic - tures you in ev - 'ry stroke. In shoot - ing
life to all, love the great, and love the small, have shown us
to your throne, serv - ing peo - ple as your own. We lift our

calm and trees of Josh - ua stand, re - flect - ing might and grace of God.
com - ets and each spark - ling star re - veals your glo - ry in deep - est space.
mer - cy's store that in our hearts your gifts of good - ness we may know.
song to you, Al - might - y God, be now our rule e - ter - nal - ly.

Psalm 29

10 Jesus, Jesus, How We Adore You

°JAI JAI YISU

C. Jadhav
Trans. by C. D. Rockey

Indian melody
As sung by D.S. Dharmapalan, 1981
°Transcr. by I-to Loh

(♩= c. 108) Introduction only ... Refrain

Je - sus, Je - sus, How we a - dore you. O Lord God, Cre-

a - tor of all, Sus - tain - er of all, Re - deem - er of

Fine

all. Je - sus, Je - sus, How we a - dore you.

1. You left the glo - ry, ful - fill - ing God's plan,
2. When we come to you in our pain,
3. Hal - le - lu - jah! Glo - ry, glo - ry!

Giv - ing your life, re - deem - ing us.
You will give us peace once a - gain,
Men and wom - en tell the sto - ry.

Dal segno al fine

O Life - giv - er, hail! O Joy - giv - er, hail!
Dis - pell - ing our gloom, re - deem - ing our doom.
Come now, one and all; come, both great and small.

Transcr. copyright © 1983 I-to Loh.
Trans. © 1983 by Mrs. Helen C. Rockey.
Performance suggestions: See #6 on page xii. No harmony to be added.
John 1:14

JESUS CHRIST

Indian

Joy Oh! Jesus, Crown of All   11

SAMAR

BINDUNATH SARKER
Trans. by MARTIN ADHIKARY
Para. by JAMES MINCHIN, 1980

Bangladesh song
Adapt. by SAMAR DAS, 1980

Refrain (♩ = 144)

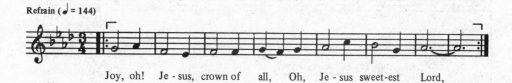

Joy, oh! Je - sus, crown of all, Oh, Je - sus sweet-est Lord,

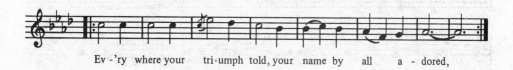

Ev - 'ry where your tri - umph told, your name by all a - dored,

Fine

Joy, oh! Je - sus, crown of all, Oh, Je - sus sweet - est Lord.

1. Love has filled our hu-man sto - ry; Peace on earth be - gins to flow-er,
2. Beat the drums and pluck the zith - er, Sing of Je - sus, Je - sus' pow-er.
3. Praise the Lord in heart-felt man - ner, Hal - le - lu - jah! This God's hour.

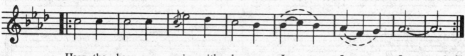

Hear the heav-ens ring with glo - ry, Joy, Joy, Joy. *(ref.)*
Wom - en chil - dren, men come hith - er, Dance for Je - sus' Joy. *(ref.)*
Greet God's Son with loud ho - san - na, Joy, Joy, Joy. *(ref.)*

Music adapt. copyright © 1983 by Samar Das.
Words copyright © 1983 by Bindunath Sarker.
Trans. copyright © 1983 by Martin Adhikary.
Para. copyright © 1983 by James Minchin.
Used by permission of the Christian Conference of Asia.
Performance suggestions: See #6 on page xii. No harmony to be added.
Philippians 2:9-11

Bangladesh   *JESUS CHRIST*

12 Lord God, Long Before Creation

HUA PEI

Anonymous, c. 1952
Trans. by Francis P. Jones, 1953

W. H. Wong, 1973

1. Lord God, long be - fore cre - a - tion You have cho - sen
2. Though the world may change its fash - ion, Yet our God is
3. God's com - pas - sion is my sto - ry, Is my boast - ing
4. Lov - ing Sav - ior now be - fore you, We will ev - er

us in love; And that love so deep, so mov - ing, Draws us close to
e'er the same, Whose com - pas - sion and whose cov'nant Through all a - ges
all the day; Mer - cy free and nev - er fail - ing, Moves my will, di -
praise your love; And our song will sound un - ceas - ing Till we reach our

Christ a - bove. Still it keeps us, still it keeps us Firm - ly fixed in
will re - main. God's own chil - dren, God's own chil - dren Must for - ev - er
rects my way. God so loved us, God so loved us, Christ the Son was
home a - bove. Giv - ing glo - ry, giv - ing glo - ry To our God and

Christ a - lone, Firm - ly fixed in Christ a - lone.
praise God's name, Must for - ev - er praise God's name.
giv'n for us, Christ the Son was giv'n for us.
to the Lamb, To our God and to the Lamb.

Ephesians 1:3-11; John 15:16

THE GOODNESS AND PROVIDENCE OF GOD

Chinese

May the Holy Spirit's Sword

JU MENG LING

Tzu-chen Chao, 1931
Trans. by Frank W. Price, 1953

Ancient Ts'ŭ melody
°Harm, AAH, 1981

Unison (♩= c. 88)

1. May the Ho - ly Spir - it's sword Pierce my soul's in - ner shield; Bid me give up all, Let me noth - ing still hoard. I yield, I yield, To Je - sus Christ my Lord.
2. May the Ho - ly Spir - it pray With word - less sighs for me; Help me in my weak - ness, Take my dis - stress a - way. I see, God's love, Christ can save me to - day.
3. May the Ho - ly Spir - it shine Like sun - light from a - bove, Drive doubt from my heart, Send his life in - to mine. God's life, I God's love, Life so great, Love di - vine.

Words and music from *Hymns of Universal Praise*, revised edition. Copyright © 1977 by the Chinese Christian Literature Council Ltd., Hong Kong.
Harm. copyright © 1983 by Abingdon Press.

Ephesians 6:17-18; Romans 8:26

Chinese

THE HOLY SPIRIT

14 O Come, Creator Spirit

ESPIRITU SANTO

V. H. FORTUNATUS
Latin, 6th century

FRANCISCO F. FELICIANO, 1980

(♩ = c. 88)

1. O come, cre - a - tor Spir - it, come
2. O Gift of God, most high, your name
3. The sev'n - fold gift of grace is yours,
4. Your light to ev - 'ry sense im - part;
5. Drive far a - way our spir - it's foe,
6. Through you may we the Fa - ther learn,

And make with - in our souls your home;
Is Com - fort - er, whom we ac - claim,
O fin - ger of the hand di - vine;
Pour forth your love on ev - 'ry heart;
Your own a - bid - ing peace be - stow;
And know the Son, and you dis - cern,

Sup - ply your grace and heav'n - ly aid
The fount of life, the fire of love,
The Fa - ther's prom - ise true, to teach
Our weak - ened flesh re - new, re - store
If you will go be - fore as guide
Who are of both, and thus a - dore

To fill the hearts which
The soul's a - noint - ing
Our earth - ly tongues - your
Our strength and cour - age
No e - vil can our
In per - fect faith for

you have made.
from a - bove.
heav'n - ly speech. A - men.
ev - er - more.
steps be - tide.
ev - er - more.

John 4:14, 14:16; Acts 2:1-4

THE HOLY SPIRIT

Filipino

O Praise the Lord

BHAGWAN

Traditional text
Adapt. and alt. by I-to Loh, 1980

Bhajan melody of India
As sung by Bishop AZARIAH
Transcr. by I-to Loh, 1980

O praise the Lord, O praise the Lord, O praise the Lord, 1. God the
2. God the
3. God the
4. God, e-

Fa - ther, Fount of Love. O praise the Lord, O praise the Lord,
Son, our Sav - ior.
Spir - it, Com-fort - er.
ter - nal Trin - i - ty.

O praise the Lord, God the Fa - ther, Fount of Love.
God the Son, our Sav - ior.
God the Spir - it, Com-fort - er.
God e - ter - nal Trin - i - ty.

Music and text copyright © 1983 by I-to Loh.

Performance suggestions:

1. *For the first stanza the leader sings each phrase (marked by double bar lines), and congregation repeats after.*
2. *From stanza 2, all sing together through the piece, without leader-chorus response.*
3. *Begin slowly, and gradually increase the dynamic and tempo from stanza 2. Slow down at stanza 4 and the Coda is sung very softly and slowly.*
4. *The ornaments with asterisk may be omitted or simplified in fast tempo.*
5. *Form* ‖: A A B :‖ A ‖: Coda :‖
     4x   4x
6. *No harmony to be added.*

Indian

Revelation 4:8

THE TRINITY

16 Our Souls Are Full of Praises

ROSEWOOD

Serafin E. Ruperto
°Trans. by Romeo del Rosario, 1981

Bernardino F. Custodio

1. Our souls are full of prais - es to you, O gra - cious God, For all the won - drous gifts You've set be - fore our eyes. We thank you for the pow'r You've plant - ed in our hearts. And we will al - ways glo - ri - fy your pre - cious love.

2. Your great - ness can be seen in the moun - tains and the wind, The wa - ter, and the land, The o - cean, and the stream. O Lord, your pow'r is great, And so our hearts will sing. We praise you, O Cre - a - tor, for ev - 'ry - thing.

3. Our hearts are cry - ing out, sing - ing prais - es un - re - strained, We of - fer thanks to you, For your e - ter - nal care. We mar - vel at your mer - cy which will nev - er fail, And prom - ise to pro - claim your great - ness ev - 'ry - where.

Psalm 8

THE GOODNESS AND PROVIDENCE OF GOD

Filipino

°Praise the Lord

°SAKURA

17

NOBUAKI HANAOKA, 1980

Traditional melody: "Sakura"
Transcr. AAH, 1981

(♩ = c. 84)

1. Praise the Lord, Praise the Lord, For the green - ness
2. Thanks to God, Thanks to God, For the gift of
3. Glo - ry to God, Glo - ry to God, For the grace of

of the trees, For the beau - ty of the flow'rs,
friends in Christ, For the church, our house of faith,
Christ, the Son, For the love of par - ent God,

For the blue - ness of the sky, For the great - ness
For the gift of won - drous love, For the gift of
For the com - fort and the strength Of the Spir - it,

of the sea; Praise the Lord, Praise the Lord,
end - less grace; Thanks to God, Thanks to God,
Ho - ly God; Glo - ry to God, Glo - ry to God,

Now and for - ev - er.
Now and for - ev - er.
Now and for - ev - er.

Performance suggestions: See #s 1, 4, and 5 on page xii.

I Peter 1:3-4; John 3:16

Japanese

THE GOODNESS AND PROVIDENCE OF GOD

18 Sing with Hearts

INTAKO

Jonathan Malicsi

Kalinga traditional melody

Sing with hearts, sing with souls, Dance with joy to God, To whom we of-fer

prais-es, to whom we sing with glad-ness.

1. Let all your hearts o-pen
2. Let all your souls shine
3. Let all your bod-ies

up to the Lord God, Let all the heav'ns hear how your hearts re-joice;
out with God's beau-ty, Let all the be-ings feel your love for God;
sway to God's mu-sic, Let all the earth move with your feet and hands;

For it is God who has giv-en us grac-es, From whom comes the
For it is God who has grant-ed us wis-dom, In whom we find re-
For it is God who in-spires and up-lifts us, From whom flows all

mu-sic in our voice. Oh, Lord, we sing with joy-ful
al-i-ty and dream.
rhy-thm in our dance.

hearts, with soul and bod-y of-fer we our arts.

Psalm 100

THE GOODNESS AND PROVIDENCE OF GOD

Filipino

Still, I Search for My God

Francisco F. Feliciano, 1977   **WASDIN PANG IPAAD**   Francisco F. Feliciano, 1977

(♩ = c. 60) With utmost simplicity

1. Still, I search for my God in silence, I mar - vel at the u - ni - verse, The world it con - tains, the beau - ty, the har - mo - ny! Cre - a - tor of such per - fec - tion, Who else could it be?
2. Come, lis - ten to the trees, the green fields, The riv - ers and the morn - ing breeze, The birds of the air all sing - ing their Mak - er's praise. Cre - a - tor of count - less won - ders, Who else could it be?
3. Yes, I am filled with peace, for I feel The pres - ence of the Lord my God. Your praise I will sing, my Mak - er, Cre - a - tor of all, Be - cause when I think of your works, Joy reigns in my heart.

Copyright © 1983 by Francisco F. Feliciano.

Filipino   *Psalm 19; I Peter 1:8*   *GOD'S CREATION*

The God of Us All

°SANTA MESA

RON O'GRADY, 1980   I-TO LOH, 1980

1. The God of us all is our Fa - ther, He guides us when we are in dan - ger, He calls us to hon - or the stran - ger, Great is the Lord Ev - er a - dored.
2. The God of us all is our Moth - er, She teach - es us her truth and beau - ty, She shows us a love be - yond du - ty,
3. Our God is a Fa - ther and Moth - er, Sur - round - ing us all with pro - tec - tion, To give to the world new di - rec - tion,

(Koto)

Music copyright © 1983 by I-to Loh.
Words copyright © 1983 by Ron O'Grady.
Performance suggestion: See #5 on page xii.

Psalm 91; Ephesians 5:1-2

THE GOODNESS AND PROVIDENCE OF GOD

Taiwanese

The Grace of God Unbounded Is   21

HOLY LOVE

Newton Y. T. Tsiang, 1931
Trans. by Frank W. Price, 1953

Ernest Y. L. Yang, 1931

Unison (♩ = c. 72)

1. The grace of God un - bound - ed is,
2. The birds they sing their Mak - er's praise,
3. God's ho - ly light sets hearts a - glow,
4. God's saints of old were brave and bold,
5. The old year goes, the new ar - rives,

All space God made, all time is his,
The stars of heav'n o - bey God's ways,
It makes more clear the way to go,
God's saints to - day firm faith must hold:
But you are still Lord of our lives:

The years roll by, God's love re - mains,
Then why should we for - get God's care?
Re - joice, my soul, and do not fear,
O Christ Di - vine, give us your pow'r,
Send us true joy, drive gloom a - way,

So thank we God, with glad re - frains.
And why should we not trust in prayer?
Now fol - low God's light, through this New Year.
That we fail not in this great hour.
Live in and through us ev - 'ry day. A - men.

Words and music from *Hymns of Universal Praise*, revised edition. Copyright © 1977 by the Chinese Christian Literature Council Ltd., Hong Kong.
Isaiah 65:17-18; II Corinthians 5:17
Chinese

THE GOODNESS AND PROVIDENCE OF GOD

22 The Smallest of My Brothers

PSALM 151

David's Psalm found in Dead Sea Scrolls
Vers. by Ivy Balchin, 1974

W. H. WONG, 1974

1. The small-est of my broth-ers, My fa-ther's young-est son, The
2. The moun-tains do not wit-ness, Nor do the hills pro-claim: The
3. With oil the proph-et blest me, T'was Sam-uel raised me high: My

flocks and calves I tend-ed, A shep-herd to be-come. My
trees God's words have cher-ished, The flock the works ac-claim. For
broth-ers fair and hand-some, The Lord God passed them by. Then

hands the strings have fash-ioned, A lyre my fin-gers wrought, "To
who can speak the won-ders, And who the deeds re-call? All
from the flock God took me, A-noint-ed me to be The

God I ren-der glo-ry," My soul with-in me thought.
things are in God's knowl-edge, And God has heed-ed all.
lead-er of the peo-ple, To rule God's chil-dren free.

I Samuel 16:1-13

THE GOODNESS AND PROVIDENCE OF GOD

Chinese

The Word Became Flesh

23

°MAHL-SEUM

Kyung Woon Choi, 1980
Para. by Elise Shoemaker, 1981

Gil Sang Kwon, 1980

(♩ = c. 104)

1. Leav-ing heav-en's glo-ry, Je-sus came to earth,
2. We are re-cre-a-ted as we re-ceive that Word;
3. When we hear God speak-ing, earth no long-er rules.
4. From God's Word comes pow-er; dark-ness is o-ver-come.
5. Since God's Word came to us, sin and death are gone.

Bring-ing all the good news: God does dwell with us.
Heal-ing sin-sick souls, God brings us life a-new.
Liv-ing with Christ as Lord brings heav'n to each new day.
As we live in wit-ness, Christ is shared in the world.
Dark-ness turns to light, God gives e-ter-nal life.

Refrain

The Word made flesh has come in Je-sus Christ the Son.

God's Word, the Son has come; our dark-ness turns to light.

Korean   John 1:14   *JESUS CHRIST*

24　°Valley Psalm to the Holy Spirit

°KATARUNGAN

MELCHIZEDEK M. SOLIS, 1979

MUTYA LOPEZ SOLIS, 1979

1. Come, Ho - ly Spir - it, come, Show us our way Through night-mare
2. Come, Ho - ly Spir - it, come, Link arms and hearts; U - nite us
3. In - spire our ris - ing youth To dream bold dreams Up - on wrath's

al - leys of our his - to - ry.
in our stand for truth and jus - tice. En - trust our chil -dren with build-er's
rub - ble and re - store com - mu - ni - ty.

vi - sion.　Em - pow'r them to soar a - bove hate bar - riers,

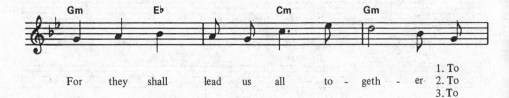

For　they　shall　lead　us　all　to - geth - er　1. To 2. To 3. To

shape　your　new　cit - y　in　our　time.
break　e - vil　dens　and　pris - on　cells
share　Christ's　true　love　for　mak - ing　peace.

John 14:16-17, 20:21-23

THE HOLY SPIRIT

Filipino

Without, Within, Above

TRINITY

Lois F. Bello, 1961, °rev., 1980

Eliseo Pajaro, 1961

1. O God, you are with - out, Your beau - ty now we praise, Your wis - dom, might, and maj - es - ty, The strength of all your ways.

2. O God, you are with - in, Your rule in us make known. De - clare your word with - in the soul And there you'll reign a - lone.

3. O God, you are a - bove, Un - search - a - ble your ways, We trace your wis - dom through your love, to you un - end - ing praise!

Refrain

God, you are ev - 'ry-where, With - out, with - in, a - bove; From morn till eve let all de - clare your glo - ry and your love.

Music copyright © 1961 by Eliseo Pajaro.
Words copyright © 1961, 1983 by Lois F. Bello.

Psalm 139:7-12

Filipino

THE GOODNESS AND PROVIDENCE OF GOD

11
The Church

An Ardent Prayer

JORGE

26

Gregorio T. Samoy, 1980

Wesley Tactay Tabayoyong, 1981

(♩ = c. 108)

1. We thank you, Lord, for our dear lives, and for the things which
2. We are be-set by pres-sures sore, In all our dai-ly
3. We pray that all peo-ple ev-'ry-where Will un-der-stand our
4. We ask you, Lord, to help pre-serve The fam-i-ly u-nit

us sus-tain, And for the op-por-tu-ni-ty
liv-ing, Lord, In work or play or an-y-where,
good in-tent To live with them in u-ni-ty,
to con-serve, That we may live in har-mo-ny,

Of com-ing to this coun-try large. Fa-ther Di-vine,
We feel that dan-ger's lurk-ing there. Fa-ther Di-vine,
That all at-tain pros-per-i-ty. Fa-ther Di-vine,
In peace and love and pur-i-ty. Fa-ther Di-vine,

We ask you, Lord, To give us grat-i-tude for all.
We ask you, Lord, To give us cour-age to en-dure.
We ask you, Lord, To give us un-der-stand-ing love.
We ask you, Lord, To give us one-ness in our homes.

Music copyright © 1983 by Wesley Tactay Tabayoyong.
Words copyright © 1983 by Gregorio T. Samoy.

Psalm 133:1

Filipino

UNITY AND FELLOWSHIP

27 All of the World God Did Create

HYOUNG-JEH

Byung Sup Ban
°Trans by T. Tom Lee
Vers. by Esther Rice; alt. AAH, 1981

Soon Jae Kim
Alt., 1981

(♩. = c. 54)

1. All of the world God did cre-ate; God the world's Mak-er cre-a-ted me, too. Now I can hear sum-mons so clear; I, the crea-ture re-spond to God's call. By the Lord a mis-sion is giv'n.

2. All of the world, all this wide world, Is a coun-try so dear to my heart. God has giv'n neigh-bors to love, Neigh-bors near and neigh-bors far. Now this mis-sion I would ac-cept

3. May we all o-ver the world Serve as one our Lord and our God. Peo-ples who dwell, o-ver the earth, Broth-ers, sis-ters, one in the Lord. Let us all one fam-i-ly be,

Music and words used by permission of the Korean Hymnal Committee.
Trans. copyright © 1983 by T. Tom Lee.
Vers. copyright © 1983 by Abingdon Press.

UNITY AND FELLOWSHIP

Korean

We would seek to re - mem-ber God's call. Joy- ful - ly live, all of our days,
From the Lord by whom I was made. Neigh-bors I'll serve, serve with love,
Joined by faith in Je - sus our Lord. Here on the earth, plant-ing God's seed,

Seek - ing in faith to o - bey God's com-mands, Joy - ful - ly live now,
With thanks-giv - ing fill - ing my heart. Neigh - bors I'll serve now,
That it may grow 'til the end of the world. Here on the earth now,

joy - ful - ly serve, We shall seek to o - bey God's com-mands.
serv - ing with love, With thanks - giv - ing fill - ing my heart.
plant - ing God's seed, May it grow 'til the end of the world.

John 1:3

28 Christ the Lord Is Risen Today

°ALLELUIA

CHARLES WESLEY, 1739, and others; alt.

WESLEY TACTAY TABAYOYONG, 1981

(♩ = c.116)

1. Christ the Lord is ris'n to - day, Al - le - lu - ia!
2. Lives a - gain our glo - rious King, Al - le - lu - ia!
3. Love's re - deem - ing work is done, Al - le - lu - ia!
4. Soar we now where Christ has led, Al - le - lu - ia!

Al - le - lu - ia! Sons of men and an - gels say,
Al - le - lu - ia! Where, O death, is now your sting?
Al - le - lu - ia! Fought the fight, the bat - tle won,
Al - le - lu - ia! Fol - l'wing our ex - alt - ed Head,

Al - le - lu - ia! Al - le - lu - ia! Raise your joys and
Al - le - lu - ia! Al - le - lu - ia! Once he died, our
Al - le - lu - ia! Al - le - lu - ia! Death in vain for -
Al - le - lu - ia! Al - le - lu - ia! Made like him, like

EASTER

Filipino

tri - umphs high, Al - le - lu - ia! God on high.
souls to save, Al - le - lu - ia! God on high.
bids him rise, Al - le - lu - ia! God on high.
him we rise, Al - le - lu - ia! God on high.

Refrain

Sing, you heav'ns, and earth re - ply,
Where's your vic - t'ry, boast - ing grave? Al - le - lu - ia! Al - le-
Christ has o - pened par - a - dise,
Ours the cross, the grave, the skies,

lu - ia! Christ the Lord is ris - en to - day! Al - le-

lu - ia! Al - le - lu - ia! Christ the Lord is ris - en to - day!

Romans 6:9, 8:34-39

29 Cold Is the Edge of the Night Wind

SISILA SULANGA

E. Walter Marasinghe
Trans. by James Minchin, 1980

E. Walter Marasinghe, 1980

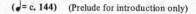

(♩ = c. 144)　(Prelude for introduction only)

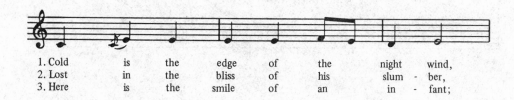

1. Cold　is　the　edge　of　the　night　wind,
2. Lost　in　the　bliss　of　his　slum - ber,
3. Here　is　the　smile　of　an　in - fant;

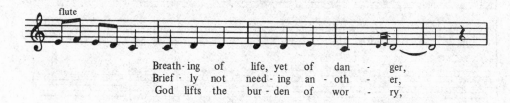

Breath - ing　of　life, yet　of　dan - ger,
Brief - ly　not　need - ing　an - oth - er,
God　lifts　the　bur - den　of　wor - ry,

Her - ald - ed　on - ly　by　star - light,
Je - sus　e - vokes　by　his　be - ing,
Hu - man　hope　finds　its　ful - fill - ment;

ADVENT AND CHRISTMAS

Sri Lankan

30

°Do You Know Me?

°BRANDEIS

Steve Chen, 1980

Tsung-hsien Yang, 1981

Andante (♩ = 66)

1. Like a strange bird who at the win-dow knocks, Or
2. Like an ex - tra who comes to meet the Board, A
3. When I come to your bus - y, sched-uled church, 'Tis

like a stran - ger who waits in the snow for a ride; I
wea - ry trav' - ler who lies in your back yard a - sleep, Un-
true no charge cards or ref - 'renc - es have I to show. When

— 3 —

touched you, e - ven at nois - y rock con-certs, in a crowd; I've
want - ed there, yet I've laughed with your chil - dren and cried; I've
you are hav - ing the Ho - ly Com - mu - nion with - in, I'm

8va

talked to you dur - ing lone - ly night.
moved that huge stone that blocked your way.
count - ing the fall - en leaves out - side.

♩ = ♩. Refrain

Do you know me by feel - ing my pains? Do you know me

tast - ing my blood? I am the one from Naz - a - reth, who's

fight - ing the whole world with love.

Music copyright © 1983 by Tsung-hsien Yang.
Words copyright © 1983 by Steve Chen.

*Performance suggestion: *May be sung unaccompanied, or with piano playing the melody in octaves.*

HOLY COMMUNION

Taiwanese

Mark 14:22-24

Hallelujah, Christ Is Risen

TINMINAGO

Francisco F. Feliciano, 1977   Francisco F. Feliciano, 1977

Not fast but with steady beat ($\quad$ = c. 88-96)

Hal - le, hal - le - lu - jah, hal - le - lu - jah!

Gongs*

(Continuing to the end)

1. See   the   splen - dor   of   the   morn - ing   full   of   won - der,
2. Wel - come, hail   the   Prince   of   glo - ry,   our   Re - deem - er.
3. Fill   our   hearts   with   faith   and   joy   of   sal - va - tion,
4. Be   u - nit - ed   in   the   name   of   Christ   our   Sav - ior,
5. Hon - or,   praise   God   who   raised   Je - sus   from   death's   pris - on;

Hear   the   good   news: Christ   is   ris - en,   Christ   is   ris - en.
Shout   with   joy,   for   he   has   freed   us,   he   has   freed   us.
That   with   Je - sus   we   may   tri - umph   in   true   glo - ry.
And   pro - claim through - out   the   world   his   res - ur - rec - tion.
Praise   be   to   the   Fa - ther,   Son,   and   Ho - ly   Spir - it.

Hal - le - lu - jah, hal - le - lu, hal - le - lu - jah!

Copyright © 1983 by Francisco F. Feliciano
Performance suggestions:
°-let instrument vibrate.
⁺-hold instrument so it does not vibrate.
*Gong rhythm continues even after vs. 5, then fades.
Gong 3 keeps steady ryhthm without changing accent.
Gongs 1 and 2 keep eighth-note rhythm but improvise by varying the accent.

Romans 6:9; Luke 24:34

Filipino   *EASTER*

33 °Holy Christmas Night

CHRISTMAS UNIVERSAL

EPPIE DURAN, 1978
Allegretto (♩ = c. 88)

EPPIE DURAN, 1978
°Harm, AAH, 1981

1. Can you hear the call of a shep-herd boy, Point-ing to a star
2. You can feel the breeze bring-ing win - ter's kiss; You can hear the song
3. Can you see a world shiv-'ring in the cold? Can you feel your heart

shin-ing from a - far? Can you hear the knock at a lone - ly door?
of a heav'n - ly throng. You can touch the hay, where the ba - by lay;
with a hope so bright? Now God's gift is here; heaven's joy is near.

Can you hear them say, "May we come to stay?" Can you see the men,
You can see the light on the man-ger bright; You can see the myrrh,
Giv - ing us God's own, great-est love is shown. Let this world re-joice,

with the gifts they bring, Com-ing to a town for a new - born king?
frankincense, and gold. You can see them kneel, shepherds young and old.
make a joy - ful noise. As in days of old, Let God's love be told.

ADVENT AND CHRISTMAS

Filipino

Oh, what a love-ly night, Ho-ly, ho-ly Christ-mas night.

Oh, heav'n-ly heav'n-ly night, Ho-ly, ho-ly Christ-mas night.

Luke 2:15; Matthew 2:9-11

In the Heavens Shone a Star 34

KALINGA

JONATHAN MALICSI and
ELLSWORTH CHANDLEE

Kalinga traditional melody

(♩ = c. 108)

1. In the heav-ens shone a star, Van-quish-ing the gloom of night, Herald - ing a won-drous
2. From the an-gels shepherds heard, The good tid-ings of his birth, And to Beth-le-hem they
3. Wise men saw the heav'n-ly sign, Journeyed far from O-rient land, Him their Lord and King to
4. Filled with wonder and with awe, At his cra-dle low we bow To a - dore the ho-ly

birth; God's own Son now comes on earth. Je - sus Christ is born to - day, Christmas Day!
sped To be - hold his man-ger bed. Je - sus Christ is born to - day, Christmas Day!
greet, Of - f'ring trea-sures at his feet. Je - sus Christ is born to - day, Christmas Day!
Child, Son of God, and yet so mild. Je - sus Christ is born to - day, Christmas Day!

Matthew 2:9

Filipino

ADVENT AND CHRISTMAS

35 In Christ There Is No East or West

°OIKOUMENE

John Oxenham, 1908
Alt., 1981

I-to Loh, 1981

1. In Christ there is no east or west, In him no south or north;
4. In Christ now meet both east and west, In him meet south and north;

But one great fel-low-ship of love Throughout the whole wide earth.
All Christ-ly souls are one in him, Throughout the whole wide earth.

2. In him shall true hearts ev-'ry-where Their high com-mu-nion find;

His serv-ice is the gold-en cord Close bind-ing all hu-man-kind.

Music copyright © 1983 by I-to Loh.
Words by John Oxenham 1852–1941. © Desmond Dunkerley.

Performance suggestions:

1. See #s 1 and 3 on page xii.
2. Sing as written, or choose only one or two of the three settings (A,B,C) for all four stanzas.

UNITY AND FELLOWSHIP

Taiwanese

1. In Christ there is no east or west,
   In him no south or north;
   But one great fellowship of love
   Throughout the whole wide earth.

2. In him shall true hearts ev'rywhere
   Their high communion find;
   His service is the golden cord
   Close binding all humankind.

3. Join hands, then, children of the faith,
   Whate'er your race may be!
   Who serves my Father as a child
   Is surely kin to me.

4. In Christ now meet both east and west,
   In him meet south and north;
   All Christly souls are one in him,
   Throughout the whole wide earth.

Ephesians 1:10; 2:13, 19

36 For the Bread Which You Have Broken

BENG-LI

Louis F. Benson, 1924
Alt., AAH

I-to Loh, 1970

(♩ = c. 76)

1. For the bread which you have bro - ken; For the wine, which
2. By this pledge that you do love us, By your gift of
3. With our saint - ed ones in glo - ry Seat - ed at the
4. In your serv - ice, Lord, de - fend us, In our hearts keep

you have poured; For the words, which you have spo - ken;
peace re - stored, By your call to heav'n a - bove us,
Lord God's board, May the church that's wait - ing for you
watch and ward, In the world where you have sent us

Now we give you thanks, O Lord.
Hal - low all our lives, O Lord.
Keep love's tie un - bro - ken, Lord.
Let your king - dom come, O Lord. A - men.

Music copyright © 1983 by I-to Loh.
Words used by permission of Robert F. Jeffreys, Jr.
Performance suggestion: See #s 1 and 3 on page xii.

Mark 14:22-24

HOLY COMMUNION

Taiwanese

Here, O Lord, Your Servants Gather 37

TŌKYŌ

Tokuo Yamaguchi, 1958
Para. by Everett M. Stowe, 1958; alt., 1972

Japanese Gagaku mode
Arr. by Isao Koizumi, 1958

1. Here, O Lord, your ser-vants gath-er, Hand we link with hand; Look-ing toward our Sav-ior's cross, Joined in love we stand. As we seek the realm of God, We u-nite to pray: Je-sus, Sav-ior, guide our steps, For you are the Way.

2. Man-y are the tongues we speak, Scat-tered are the lands, Yet our hearts are one in God, One in love's de-mands. E'en in dark-ness hope ap-pears, Call-ing age and youth: Je-sus, teach-er, dwell with us, For you are the Truth.

3. Na-ture's se-crets o-pen wide, Chan-ges nev-er cease; Where, O where, can wea-ry souls Find the source of peace? Un-to all those sore dis-tressed, Torn by end-less strife: Je-sus, heal-er, bring your balm, For you are the Life.

4. Grant, O God, an age re-newed, Filled with death-less love, Help us as we work and pray, Send us from a-bove Truth and cour-age, faith and power Need-ed in our strife: Je-sus Mas-ter, be our Way, Be our truth, our life.

Performance suggestion: See #s 2, 4, and 5 on page xii.

John 14:6; Romans 10:12-13; Ephesians 1:7-14

Japanese

UNITY AND FELLOWSHIP

38 In This World Abound Scrolls of Wisdom

MŌSŌ

Saichirō Yuya, before 1903; alt.
Trans. by Esther Hibbard, 1963

Old Japanese melody of Chinese origin
As adapted in "Sambika," 1954
Harm. by Kazu Nakaseko, 1963

Unison (♩ = c. 56)

1. In this world a-bound Scrolls of wis-dom num-ber-less,
2. Stud-y as we may, Nev-er can we grasp there-by

But the pur-est truth In the Word of God is found;
All the depth of truth; We must ev-er watch and pray,

This the book that points the way Trod by the sa-ges long a-go.
Walk-ing on the ho-ly way Trod by the sa-ges long a-go.

Words used by permission of the Japanese Hymnal Committee.
Harm. used by permission of Kiyoaku Sumiya.
Performance suggestion: See #s 1, 4 on page xii.

II Timothy 3:14-17; John 17:17; Jeremiah 9:23, 24; 1 Corinthians 2:12, 13

THE HOLY SCRIPTURES

Japanese

I'll Shout the Name of Christ Who Lives 39

°BAHAY KUBO

Vivincio L. Vinluan, 1980

(♩ = c. 126)

Wesley Tactay Tabayoyong, 1981
Motive from Philippine folksong "Bahay Kubo"

1. I'll shout the name of Christ who lives, He
2. Dear broth - ers sing a - mong stran - gers here, And
3. Once more we shout our joy and praise To the

lives, He lives, that I might live a - gain, He
leap with joy, my sis - ters dear; A -
Lord we love, whose throne is grace, Whose

broke death's pow'r at Cal - va - ry, And
lone at home we seek our peace, There
way is Life, whose word is ful - filled As

now I know from sin I'm free.
Je - sus comes to bring re - lease.
we in glad - ness do God's will.

Romans 6:5-11

Filipino

EASTER

40 Jesus Has Come to Earth

AYA HAI, YISHU

Trans. by the Rev. A. G. ATKINS

Indian melody
Transcr. by the Rev. and Mrs. A. G. ATKINS

Refrain (Repeat only for introduction)

(♩ = c. 100)

Fine

Je-sus has come to earth, Je-sus has come! Bring-ing sal-va - tion to all; He has come!

Verse

1. O'er hill and dale hap-py an - gels are sing - ing,
2. Though it was night, shep-herds quick - ly went to see
3. From east-ern coun - tries came al - so wise men,
4. First in Je - ru - sa - lem they in - quired ear-nest-ly,
5. At length in Beth - le - hem find - ing Mes - si - ah,
6. Hear - ing of Je - sus' love, this hum - ble ser - vant,

"Hail to the Lord! Glo - ry! Hail to the Lord!"
By an - gels' word in - spired, by an - gels' word.
Led by a star, plain - ly, led by a star,
"Where is the home, O King, Where is the home
Gold, in - cense, myrrh they bring; gold, in - cense, myrrh,
Bod - y and soul, dear friends, bod - y and soul

D.C.

With peace and good will to all, he has come.
"As son of Ma - ry, the Lord Christ is born."
Seek - ing the place where Lord Je - sus was born.
In which sal - va - tion's great King has been born?"
Of - f'ring to him, who a King has been born.
Yield - ed to him and has thus been re - born.

Music transcr. and trans. copyright © 1983 by the Rev. and Mrs. A. G. Atkins.
Performance suggestions: See #6 on page xii. No harmony to be added.

Matthew 2:1-2

ADVENT AND CHRISTMAS

Indian

Now, Let Us Sing a New Song to the Lord 41

KAMITAKATA

Naoi Ishida, 1966
° Trans. by Nobuaki Hanaoka, 1980

Isao Koizumi, 1967

1. Now, let us sing a new song to the Lord; Make a joy-ful noise with the spir-its high. To-geth-er we sing, for the new age has dawned, A new age of love and trust, new age of love and trust.

2. Now, let us sing a new song to the Lord; The song of joy-ful peo-ple of the Lord's new day. With the Word of God, pow'r-ful and so might-y, The old age of strife is gone, old age of strife is gone.

3. Now, let us sing a new song to God's praise; We lift our voic-es to the God of these new days. Till the day will come, when the Word of God Will cov-er this world of ours, cov-er this world of ours.

Music by Isao Koizumi; used by permission of JASRAC, license no. 8211927.
Words used by permission of Naoi Ishida; copyright assigned to the Japanese Hymnal Committee.
Trans. copyright © 1983 by Nobuaki Hanaoka.

Japanese

Psalm 96:1; Colossians 3:16; II Corinthians 5:17

WORSHIP AND PRAISE

42 Midnight Stars Make Bright the Sky

HUAN-SHA-CH'I

CHING-CHIU YANG, 1930
Trans. by MILDRED A. WIANT, c. 1966

CHI-FANG LIANG, 1934
Harm. by BLISS WIANT, 1934
Alt. by PEN-LI CHEN, 1981

Unison (♩ = c. 92)

1. Mid - night stars make bright the skies, Beth - le - hem in
2. Mid - night slum - ber lies o'er all, One lone bright lamp
3. Wise - men long fore - told the way, Saw the strange star's
4. God from me sin sep - a - rates, Sin's with - in, faith

slum - ber lies; Glis - t'ning heav'n sends forth great light,
lights the stall. Choose old cloth - ing, wrap him warm - ly,
shin - ing ray, Knew a child was born in Jew - ry,
dis - si - pates. I am prone to dev - il - ish ways,

Shep - herds see a won - drous sight! An - gel ranks in cho - rus sing,
Man - ger shall his cra - dle be. Will'd to save from Sa - tan's heel,
Wor - ship would be joy for aye! Took strong cam-els hur - ry - ing,
Wan - der hope - less in a maze. God's Good Shep-herd cares for me,

Silk - en sounds from heav - en ring. Fright - ened shep-herds hear them say:
Word made flesh, God's truth re - vealed, Came as man from heav - en's throne,
Cross - ing des - ert sought their King, Rev' - rent - ly to him pre - sent
How can I a lost sheep be? My clean heart shall be his throne,

Words and music from *Hymns of Universal Praise*, revised edition. Copyright © 1977 by the Chinese Christian Literature Council Ltd., Hong Kong.
Music alt. copyright © 1983 by Pen-li Chen.

ADVENT AND CHRISTMAS

Chinese

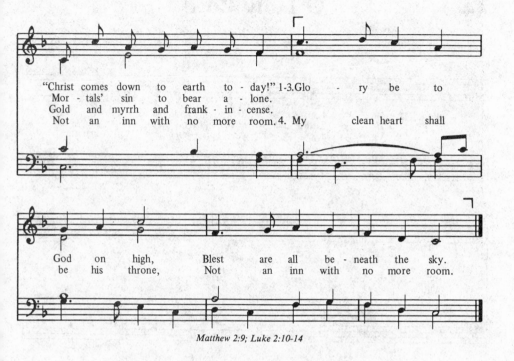

"Christ comes down to earth to - day!" 1-3.Glo - ry be to
Mor - tals' sin to bear a - lone.
Gold and myrrh and frank - in - cense.
Not an inn with no more room. 4. My clean heart shall

God on high, Blest are all be - neath the sky.
be his throne, Not an inn with no more room.

Matthew 2:9; Luke 2:10-14

Jesus Came into the World 43

APOMIN

JONATHAN MALICSI
ELLSWORTH CHANDLEE

Kalinga traditional melody

(♩= c. 92)

1. Je - sus came in - to the world as a lit - tle babe. He came,
2. Chil - dren sing - ing, church bells ring - ing, joy shines bright in ev - 'ry eye,
3. Let the skies with song re - sound - ing, each re - e - cho now with praise,
4. Our Je - sus born to - day, the world you came to save,

Bring - ing peace and hope and joy, God's great gift to hu - man - kind.
Ta - bles la - den, fam - 'lies gath - ered, for this is Christ-mas day.
Crea-tures all join the cho - rus, Glo - ry be to God.
Glo - ry now we give to you, great-est gift the Lord has giv'n.

Luke 2:16; John 1:9

Filipino

ADVENT AND CHRISTMAS

44

O Holy Lord

HOPE

HOPE KAWASHIMA, 1976

HOPE KAWASHIMA, 1976

(♩ = c. 100)

1. O Ho - ly Lord, we sing your maj - es - ty,
3. O Ho - ly Lord, we hum - bly plead with you,
4. O Ho - ly Lord, our deep - est grat - i - tude

We lift our hearts in joy - ous ec - sta - sy!
For - give our sins and all the wrong we do,
With praise to you in song we do in - clude!

Grant us your mer - cy and your grace;
Our fool - ish ways and sel - fish pride,
Lord of our life, Mas - ter sub - lime,

In faith we come be - fore your face.
So we may in your love a - bide!
Guide us and bless us through all time. A - men.

International copyright, 1976 by Hope Kawashima. By permission only.

Psalms 50; 103

WORSHIP AND PRAISE

Japanese

O Many People of All Lands

MATERNIDAD

45

NATTY G. BARRANDA, 1980

LOIS F. BELLO, 1981

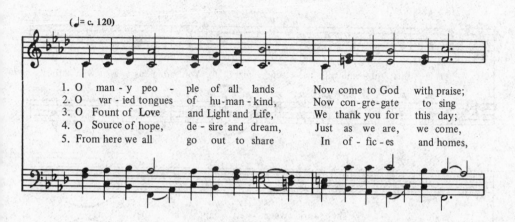

1. O man-y peo - ple of all lands   Now come to God   with praise;
2. O var - ied tongues of hu-man-kind,   Now con-gre-gate   to sing
3. O Fount of Love and Light and Life,   We thank you for   this day;
4. O Source of hope, de - sire and dream,   Just as we are,   we come,
5. From here we all go out to share   In of - fic - es   and homes,

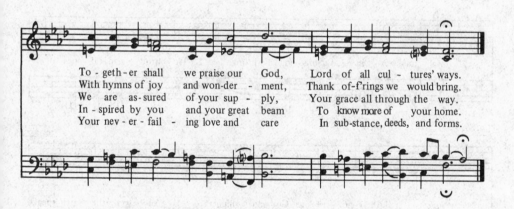

To - geth-er shall we praise our   God,   Lord of all cul - tures' ways.
With hymns of joy and won-der - ment,   Thank of-f'rings we would bring.
We are as-sured of your sup - ply,   Your grace all through the way.
In - spired by you and your great beam   To know more of your home.
Your nev - er - fail - ing love and care   In sub-stance, deeds, and forms.

Psalm 100

Filipino

UNITY AND FELLOWSHIP

46 °O Soft, Solemn Stillness of Night

HIMIG PASKO

Lois F. Bello

S. Y. Ramos
° Harm. by Lois F. Bello, 1980

(♩.= c. 52)

1. O soft sol-emn still-ness of night, You bring us a won-drous sight! The world watch-es rapt in the song of an-gels in God's shin-ing throng. 2. "We bring glad tid-ings of joy, All glo-ry to God on high, And on the earth speak

(of joy) (on high)

Melody copyright © by S. Y. Ramos.
Words and harm. copyright © 1983 by Lois F. Bello.

ADVENT AND CHRISTMAS

Filipino

peace, Good - will that will nev - er cease."

3. Sing, choirs of heav - en and earth, Ex - tol him of low - ly

birth. Christ Je - sus with us to dwell,

Our Lord Em - man - u - el, Our Lord Em - man - u - el.

Luke 2:8-14

47 Our Church Now Is Self-Reliant

INDEPENDENCE

Pao-yuan Chu, 1933
Trans. by Ivy Balchin, 1976

K. C. Wong, 1934
Harm. by Bliss Wiant, 1934

1. Our church now is self-re-li-ant, Chris-tians must their strength ex-ert:
2. Spir-it-filled, our church u-nit-ed Bear-ing bur-dens, all as one,
3. May Christ come to guide his cho-sen, To a-chieve we must u-nite,

Quick-ly sound the gos-pel trum-pet, Call-ing us to be a-lert.
O-ver-com-ing ev-'ry hin-drance, Will a force-ful church be-come.
With one heart co-op-er-a-ting, Swift-ly act like birds in flight.

Let us join hands, be u-nit-ed, Our thoughts shall be in ac-cord,
Free from ri-tual, warm in spir-it, Where prayer ris-es, Christ is there,
When God's own church is es-tab-lished, Al-le-lu-ias shall re-sound,

One in heart, in strength ad-vanc-ing, Chris-tians joined in deed and word.
Free and e-qual, peace-ful, lov-ing, All earth shall his glo-ry share.
Self sup-port-ing, prop-a-gat-ing, All to Christ for-ev-er bound.

Judges 4:14; Ephesians 6:10-20

UNITY AND FELLOWSHIP

Chinese

The Savior's Precious Blood

HYOP-TONG

Korean hymn
Trans. by WILLIAM SCOTT and YUNG WOON KIM
Alt., 1981

TAE JOON PARK

1. The Savior's precious blood Has made all nations one; United let us praise this deed The love of God has done.
2. In this vast human world, So dark and full of sin, No other theme can be our prayer Than this your kingdom come.
3. In this sad world of war, Can peace be ever found? Unless the love of Christ prevail True peace will not abound.
4. The Master's new command Is "Love each other well." O brothers, sisters, let's unite To do his holy will.

Music and words used by permission of the Korean Hymnal Committee.

John 13:34-35; 17:21; I Peter 1:18-22

Korean

UNITY AND FELLOWSHIP

49   Send Your Word

MIKOTOBA

Yasushige Imakoma, 1965
°Trans. by Nobuaki Hanaoka, 1980

Shōzō Koyama, 1965

(♩ = c. 72)

1. Send your Word, O Lord, like the rain, Fall-ing down up-on the earth. Send your Word. We seek your, end-less grace, With souls that hun-ger and thirst, Sor-row and ag-o-nize. We would all be lost in dark

2. Send your Word, O Lord, like the wind, Blow-ing down up-on the earth. Send your Word. We seek your won-drous pow'r, Pure-ness that re-jects all sins, Though they per-sist and cling. Bring us to com-plete vic-t'ry;

3. Send your Word, O Lord, like the dew, Com-ing gent-ly up-on the hills. Send your Word. We seek your end-less love. For life that suf-fers in strife With ad-ver-si-ties and hurts, Send your heal-ing pow'r of love;

Music and words used by permission of the Japanese Hymnal Committee.
Trans. copyright © by Nobuaki Hanaoka.

THE HOLY SCRIPTURES

Japanese

With - out your guid - ing light.
Set us all free in - deed.
We long for your new world. A - men.

Matthew 8:8; Amos 8:11

Word of the Lord 50
KIYOKI FUMI

TOYOHIKO KAGAWA
° Trans. by FRANK Y. OHTOMO, 1981

NAOTADA YAMAMOTO, 1976
Harm. by ISAO SAKABAYASHI, 1976

(♩ = c. 96)

Wip - ing a - way the tears, Fal - len on a leaf of the Book,

Clear - ing my eyes to read What a Word of the Lord of the Cross!

1.
What a strength of bless - ed - ness!
2.
bless - ed - ness!

Music used by permission of Naotada Yamamoto.
Words used by permission of Sumimoto Kagawa.
Trans. copyright © 1983 by Frank Y. Ohtomo.
Performance suggestion: See #s 4 and 5 on page xii.

I Corinthians 1:18

Japanese

THE HOLY SCRIPTURES

51   Silent Night! Holy Night!

˚IO-NÂ-KOA

JOSEPH MOHR, 1818

Not too slow (♩ = c. 69)

Taiwanese cradle song
Arr. by TSUNG-HSIEN YANG, 1980

1. Si - lent night! ho - ly night!   All is calm, all is
2. Si - lent night! ho - ly night!   Shep - herds quake at the
3. Si - lent night! ho - ly night!   Son of God, love's pure
4. Si - lent night! ho - ly night!   Won - drous star, lend your

bright,   Si - lent night! ho - ly night!
sight,   Si - lent night! ho - ly night!
light,   Si - lent night! ho - ly night!
light,   Si - lent night! ho - ly night!

All is calm, all is bright,   Round yon vir - gin mother and
Shep - herds quake at the sight,   Glo - ries stream from heaven a -
Son of God, love's pure light,   Radiant beams from your ho - ly
Won - drous star, lend your light,   With the an - gels let us

Arr. copyright © 1983 by Tsung-hsien Yang.

Performance suggestion: See #s 1 and 3 on page xii.

ADVENT AND CHRISTMAS

Taiwanese

child!
far,
face,
sing,

Ho - ly in-fant, so ten - der and mild,
Heav - en - ly hosts sing: "Al - le - lu - ia,
With the dawn of re - deem - ing grace,
Al - le - lu - ia to our King;

Sleep in heaven-ly peace,
Christ the Sav - ior is born,
Je - sus, Lord, at your birth,
Christ the Sav - ior is born,

Sleep in heav-en-ly peace.
Christ the Sav - ior is born.
Je - sus, Lord at your birth.
Christ the Sav - ior is born.

Matthew 2:1-2; Luke 2:8-14

52 The Sun Is Rising O'er the World

CHRISTMAS DAY

Shinsen Sambika, 1890
° Trans. by HIDEMI ITŌ
and SANDRA FUKUNAGA, 1981

CHŪGORŌ TORII, 1953

1. The Sun is ris - ing o'er the world To shed its light a - bun - dant; E'en
2. The strength and light of God's own son Brings ev - er - last - ing love; To
3. The Lord who brings sal - va - tion Was born in - to this world. Come,

those who live a - midst the dark Shall find the light comes through. The
all the earth, both great and small, God's won - drous light is shone. He
cel - e - brate, you rich and poor, And share the joy of God. The

Lord, all - know - ing, shares his strength With those a - round the world. The
gives us com - fort, cheer, and might, To share with one an - oth - er. The
Lord who rules the world has come; He guides us ev - 'ry day. Re -

meek, the hum - ble, and the lame, The light of Christ's for you.
weak, the shy, the suf - f'ring crowd, They shall be lift - ed up.
joice and lift your voic - es high, Ho - san - na, Christ our Lord.

Words and music used by permission of the Japanese Hymnal Committee.
Trans. copyright © 1981 by Hidemi Ito and Sandra Fukunaga.

John 1:4, 5, 9

ADVENT AND CHRISTMAS

Japanese

°Why Has God Forsaken Me? 53

°SHIMPI

BILL WALLACE

TAIHEI SATO, 1981

1. "Why has God for - sak - en me?" Cried our Sav - ior
2. At the tomb of Laz - a - rus Je - sus wept with
3. As his life ex - pired, our Lord Placed him - self with -
4. Mys - t'ry shrouds our life and death But we need not

from the cross As he shared the lone - li - ness
o - pen grief: Grant us, Lord, the tears which heal
in God's care: At our dy - ing, Lord, may we
be a - fraid, For the mys - t'ry's heart is love,

Of our deep - est grief and loss.
All our pain and un - be - lief.
Trust the love which con - quors fear.
God's great love which Christ dis - played.

Music copyright © 1983 by Taihei Sato.

Words from *Something to Sing About* (1981), Bill Wallace. Published by the Joint Board of Christian Education of Australia and New Zealand. Used with permission.

Performance suggestion: See #s 4 and 5 on page xii.

Matthew 27:46; John 11:35; Luke 23:46

Japanese

LENT AND PASSION

III

The Christian Life

A Hymn of Human Rights

KONG-EUI

Fred Kaan

Song Soo Kwak

(♩ = c. 92)

1. For the heal-ing   of the na-tions, Lord, we pray with   one ac-cord;
2. Lead us, Fa-ther,   in-to free-dom, From de-spair your   world re-lease;
3. All that kills a - bun-dant liv-ing, Let it from the   earth be banned;
4. You, Cre-a-tor   God, have writ-ten Your great name on   all man-kind;

For   a   just   and   e-qual shar-ing   Of the things that   earth af-fords.
That re-deemed from war and ha-tred Men may come and   go in peace.
Pride of sta-tus,   race, or school-ing. Dog-mas keep-ing   man from man.
For our grow-ing   in your like-ness Bring the life of   Christ to mind;

To   a   life   of   love in ac-tion Help us rise and   pledge our word.
Show us   how through care and good-ness Fear will   die and   hope in-crease.
In our com-mon   quest for jus-tice May we hal-low   life's brief span.
That by   our   re-sponse and serv-ice Earth its des-ti-   ny may find.

To   a   life   of   love in ac-tion Help us rise and   pledge our word.
Show us   how through care and good-ness Fear will die and   hope in-crease.
In our com-mon   quest for jus-tice May we hal-low   life's brief span.
That by   our   re-sponse and serv-ice Earth its des-ti-   ny may find.

Amos 5:24

Korean

JUSTICE AND HUMAN RIGHTS

55 Ah, What Shame I Have to Bear

IMAYŌ

SŌGO MOTSUMOTO, 1895
Trans. by ESTHER HIBBARD, 1962

12th-century Japanese melody
Arr. by KAZU NAKASEKO, 1963

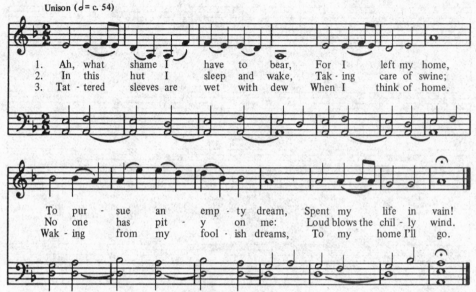

1. Ah, what shame I have to bear, For I left my home,
2. In this hut I sleep and wake, Tak-ing care of swine;
3. Tat-tered sleeves are wet with dew When I think of home.

To pur - sue an emp-ty dream, Spent my life in vain!
No one has pit - y on me: Loud blows the chil - ly wind.
Wak - ing from my fool - ish dreams, To my home I'll go.

Words and music used by permission of the Japanese Hymnal Committee. Arr. by permission of Kiyoaku Sumiya.
Performance suggestion: See #s 2 and 5 on page xii.

Luke 15:11-21

LOVE AND REPENTANCE   *Japanese*

56 Oh, the Eyes of Christ the Lord

SHU NO HITOMI

TOSHIO IOKI and SHINJI UMEDA, 1951
Trans. by NOBUAKI HANAOKA, 1980

SAHOMI TAKADA, 1952

1. Oh, the eyes of Christ the Lord, Full of com-pas-sion and
2. Oh, the eyes of Christ the Lord, Full of com-pas-sion and
3. Oh, the eyes of Christ the Lord, Full of com-pas-sion and
4. Christ to - day and yes - ter-day, With his un - chang - ing

Words and music used by permission of the Japanese Hymnal Committee.
Trans. copyright © 1983 by Nobuaki Hanaoka.

LOVE AND REPENTANCE   *Japanese*

love!
love!
love!
love;

E - ven to the wealth - y youth,
Pierc - ing through the fee - ble heart —
"Doubt - ing Thom - as, Come and see
Call - ing with his wound - ed hands,

Who walked a - way from him,
Pe - ter's heart of rock,
Scars of lance and nails.
"My dear friends, re - turn!"

Sad - dened, though, and filled with tears,
Who de - nied the Lord a - gain,
Touch and be - lieve; I love you still,"
Christ a - waits; be - hold his eyes;

Yet for - giv - ing still.
Yet for - giv - en still.
Said his lov - ing eyes.
Place your faith in him.

Christ the Mas - ter,
Yes, the Lord, our
Yes, it's you who've
Yes, it is your

in your eyes, Your pa - tient love we see.
Mas - ter Christ, Your eyes for - give us still.
come to save In your love di - vine.
eyes, O Christ, That in - vite us still.

Luke 22:61-62; John 20:27

57 Altar on Mt. Moriah

MORIAHT-SAHN

SUNG MOON PARK
°Trans. by T. TOM LEE
Vers. by ESTHER RICE, 1981

SO WOON OH
°Alt., 1981

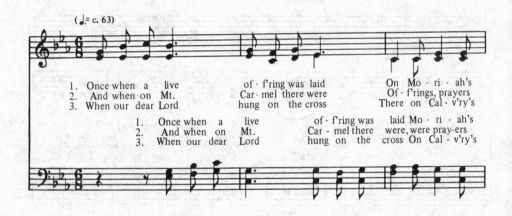

(♩. = c. 63)

1. Once when a live of - f'ring was laid On Mo - ri - ah's
2. And when on Mt. Car - mel there were Of - f'rings, prayers
3. When our dear Lord hung on the cross There on Cal - v'ry's

1. Once when a live of - f'ring was laid Mo - ri - ah's
2. And when on Mt. Car - mel there were, were pray-ers
3. When our dear Lord hung on the cross On Cal - v'ry's

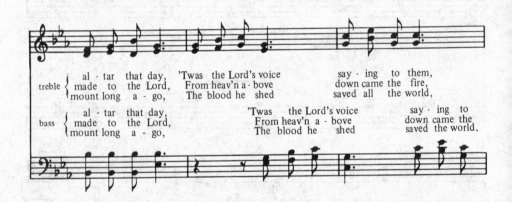

treble
al - tar that day, 'Twas the Lord's voice say - ing to them,
made to the Lord, From heav'n a - bove down came the fire,
mount long a - go, The blood he shed saved all the world,

bass
al - tar that day, 'Twas the Lord's voice say - ing to
made to the Lord, From heav'n a - bove down came the
mount long a - go, The blood he shed saved the world,

STEWARDSHIP

Korean

treble
"A   new   fount   of   bless - ing I'll   give." This fount was re -
Then that pour - ing   rain   of   God's grace. Our Lord is   the
Men   and   wom - en   of   ev - 'ry   race.   Res - ur - rect - ed,

bass
them, "New fount   of   bless - ing I'll give."
fire, that pour - ing   rain   of God's grace.
Men   and   wom - en   of   ev - 'ry race.

ceived   as   a   free   Price - less   gift   from God's gra - cious love.
true   liv - ing   Lord,   In   him   on - ly   do   we   be - lieve.
Lord Je - sus Christ   Reigns as   King   of   kings ev - er - more.

When to Mt. Mo - ri - ah we come, Let's all give our   hearts to God.
Let   us   at   the   ta - ble now kneel, Ded - i - cat - ing our-selves to God.
Let   us each ac - cept our own cross; Bear it for the   glo - ry of God.

Genesis 22:2; I Kings 18:20-38; Luke 23:32-49

58 A Lonely Boat Set Out to Sea

BAI

Helen Kim, 1921
°Trans. by Hae Jong Kim, 1980
Vers. by Linda and Doug Sugano, 1981

Dong Hoon Lee, 1967
°Alt. AAH, 1981

(♩.= c. 69)

1. A lone-ly boat set out to sea On a storm-y night;
2. The wind a-rose in its rage Toss-ing the ti-ny boat;
3. Trem-bling with fear in de-spair, Look-ing and hop-ing for help,
4. I ask for your mer-cy, O Lord, In a sin-ner like me;
5. The winds and waves, cru-el and cold, Sure-ly may rise a-gain;

The cru-el sea seemed so wide, The waves so high.
The bil-lows high, high-er they grew, O-ver the boat.
The sail-or thought strength and hope Come from a-bove.
Com-mand, O Lord, to be calm The wind and sea.
Threat-en-ing boats, threat-en-ing lives On the wide sea.

This sin-gle ship sailed the sea, In-to the gale;
The sail-or stood all a-lone, Won-d'ring what to do;
God will be there in the boat, Stand-ing by his side.
Grant un-to me a new hope For a new life;
Pow'r-ful and great is God's hand In firm con-trol;

Oh, great is the per-il, Great is the per-il.
Oh, so help-less is he, So help-less is he.
Oh, seek now the Sav-ior, Seek now the Sav-ior.
Oh, be mer-ci-ful, Lord, Be mer-ci-ful, Lord.
Oh, peace comes from you, Lord, Peace comes from you, Lord.

Music and words used by permission of the Korean Hymnal Committee.
Trans. copyright © 1983 by Hae-Jong Kim.
Vers. copyright © 1983 by Linda and Doug Sugano.

Mark 4:35-41

CHRISTIAN EXPERIENCE AND DEVOTION

Korean

Beyond Loud Protestations

°KAPAYAPAAN

Melchizedek M. Solis, 1981

Mutya Lopez Solis, 1981

1. Be - yond loud pro - tes - ta - tions, A - bove the clash of castes,
2. We heed the hun - gry cry - ing In pain from fu - rious wants;
3. We pray you'll give the Life Source, Our shield a - gainst the foe

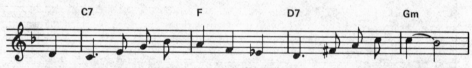

O'er vio - lent dem - on - stra - tions A - gainst a - buse and lusts,
The rich are damned to griev - ing, Pris - 'ners to death's own taunts.
As pil - grims on the peace course The way of Christ we know,

Your rec - on - cil - i - a - tion Draws ri - val hearts a - round,
With songs of lib - er - a - tion, Re - leased from chains of greed,
Like him our goals are bridg - es O'er cha - sms gouged by wars,

Break - ing bread and cel - e - bra - tion With en - e - mies, love bound.
With you from death's dam - na - tion, We march as sin - ners freed.
We scale Gol - go - tha's ridg - es, Bear cross and shame and scars.

II Corinthians 5:17-21

Filipino

JUSTICE AND HUMAN RIGHTS

60 Celebrating God's Reign

GÛ-LÊ-KOA

Fred Kaan

Based on Taiwanese folksong,
"Gû-lê-koa"
I-to Loh, 1980

Unison (♩ = c. 100)

1. We long to learn to praise, In si - lence and in
2. Let wor-ship come to life In hum - ble frame of
3. Give us your line to learn And prompt us in with

tone; To wor-ship you in man - y ways, To - geth - er and a-
mind, In our ap-proach to men and things And in our use of
role Of be - ing man with men on earth, To love with heart and

lone. Lord, teach us where and how To
time. Lord, you de - sire our praise In
soul. Help us to live and sing The

Music copyright © 1983 by I-to Loh.

Performance suggestion: See #s 1 and 3 on page xii.

DAILY LIFE   *Taiwanese*

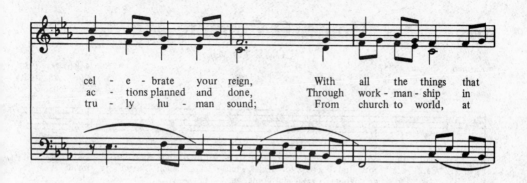

cel - e - brate your reign, With all the things that
ac - tions planned and done, Through work - man - ship in
tru - ly hu - man sound; From church to world, at

come to hand, In col - or and de - sign.
dai - ly task, In lei - sure time and fun.
home, at work, In our un - bro - ken round.

John 4:23-24

61 Come, O Come to Me

COME TO ME

Kanjirō Nagasaka, 1951
Trans. by Vern Rossman

Shōzō Koyama, 1952
Alt., 1981

(♩ = c. 100)

1. Plod - ding on, the wea - ry foot-steps through the des - ert wend,
2. Bare of foot and cold of heart, what can such suf - f'ring mend?
3. Ev - er cir - cling, seek - ing home, yet nev - er an - y - where;

Emp - ty sands and burn - ing waste - land, lone - li - ness no end;
Thirst in - tense with - out as - suage-ment brings life near its end.
Death seems near, and death seems friend - ly, such is life's de - spair.

Then his voice comes gent - ly with a whis-pered ur - gent plea,
But there comes his gen - tle call - ing, light as morn - ing dew,
At that mo - ment, God speaks clear - ly, from high heav - en's gates,

"Come now, friend, and cease your wan - d'ring; come, O come to me."
"Come and drink from Life's pure foun - tain; here it flows for you."
"Come back chil - dren, all my chil - dren; Lo your Par - ent waits."

Words and music used by permission of the Japanese Hymnal Committee.

Matthew 11:28; John 14:18

CHRISTIAN EXPERIENCE AND DEVOTION

Japanese

Drawing Near and List'ning

SOH-MYOUNG

62

BYUNG SOO OH
°Trans. by T. TOM LEE
Vers. by ESTHER RICE; alt. AAH, 1981

WOON YOUNG RA

(♩= c. 69)

1. Draw-ing near and list'n-ing, we can hear God's call;
2. In the com-ing of the Sav-ior good news was pro-claimed;
3. We will live with those whose lives are filled with deep-est pain.

As our hearts re-spond we seek to fol-low our Guide.
In the com-ing of Christ Je-sus, God's love was shown.
We will live with peo-ple who are hun-gry, who thirst.

Then will our com-mit-ment to our God deep-er grow, And
For e-ter-ni-ty we hold a hope now as-sured, And
We will live in hum-ble ways as neigh-bor to all, And

we live as those who pray a path-way to know.
we live as those who seek a wit-ness for our Lord.
we live as those who seek to be as Christ, in love.

Matthew 16:24

Korean

CHRISTIAN MISSION AND CONCERN

63   Fount of Love, Our Savior God

°MAN-CHIANG-HUNG

ERNEST Y. L. YANG, 1934
Trans. by FRANK W. PRICE, 1953
°Alt., 1981

Ancient Chinese verse tune
Adapt. by ERNEST Y. L. YANG, 1933
Alt. and arr. by I-TO LOH, 1981

Unison (♩ = c. 84)

1. Fount of love, our Sav - ior God, Light on baf - fling
2. In this age of sore dis - tress Hid - den dan - gers
3. In this chang - ing world of care Dreams like bub - bles
4. Man - y paths be - fore us lie, Man - y voic - es
5. To this earth of gloom and night, You did bring true

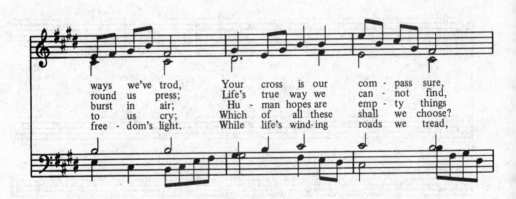

ways we've trod, Your cross is our com - pass sure,
round us press; Life's true way we can - not find,
burst in air; Hu - man hopes are emp - ty things
to us cry; Which of all these shall we choose?
free - dom's light. While life's wind - ing roads we tread,

DAILY LIFE

Chinese

Your love keeps our vi - sion pure. Lord, we thank you
Dis - il - lu - sion fills the mind. Sav - ior, give us
Like dead trees and dried - up springs. Help us, Christ our
Here find peace or there all lose? Je - sus, take our
Shep - herd Christ, lead on a - head. Guide us through the

for your grace; Dark - ness flees be - fore your face.
eyes to see Your great king - dom that will be.
Lord, we pray, Send us new life ev - 'ry day.
hands, we pray, Show us your di - vine true way.
nar - row door To your joy for - ev - er - more.

Refrain

Fount of love, our Sav - ior God, Be our Guide. A - men.

Psalm 46; Romans 8:35-39

64 Go Forth

CRUSADES—MANILA

Viola Rich Smith

Viola Rich Smith
Alt., 1981

(♩ = c. 120)   Descant

3. Go forth! Go   forth   in pa - tience, dai - ly   liv - ing

1. Go   forth!   Go   forth   in mer - cy to re - veal him,
2. Make known!   Make known   his   gra - cious in - vi - ta - tion
(Unison) 3. Go   forth!   Go   forth   in   pa - tience dai - ly   liv - ing

The   gos - pel   truth,   trans - form - ing lives of   sin

The Lord   who   came   all   na - tions to re - deem,
For peo - ple ev - 'ry where to find re - lease
The   gos - pel   truth,   trans - form - ing lives of   sin

CHRISTIAN MISSION AND CONCERN

Filipino

To glo-rious lights of Christ's cre - a - tion,

That they who know not Christ may find him;
From sin's do - min - ion wild with ha - treds;
To glo - rious lights of Christ's cre - a - tion,

The chil - dren of God he died on earth to win. A - men.

Their lives made righ-teous in God's own es - teem.
And bring sad hearts to find in love his peace.
The chil - dren of God he died on earth to win. A - men.

Acts 1:8

65 Harvest Thanksgiving

KAHM-SAH

OK IN LIM, 1967
°Trans. by HAE JONG KIM, 1980

JAE HOON PARK, 1967

1. All moun-tains are a-burn-ing with fall's col - ors bright;
2. Ev - 'ry field is so fer - tile that it har - vest bears;
3. Ear - ly spring, all the farm-ers went and sowed their seed,
4. Let us then go on sow - ing as our seed, God's Word;

The val - leys are all full of wa - ter that gives life.
Each or - chard is full of the love - ly, ripe new fruits.
They la - bored; with all their toil they pre - pared their ground.
He will send both dew and rain that the seeds may sprout.

Gold - en grain tells us of the plen - ti - ful har - vest;
Rain and sun in their time came, thus the Lord de - signed.
Their re - ward is the joy of har - vest so plen - teous;
When the land seems all bar - ren, let us not give up;

Sky - ward rise, so beau - ti - ful, all the songs of praise.
The la - bor of hands has brought all this har - vest joy.
Prom - ised bless - ings will be theirs on the har - vest day.
We will wait for har - vest time, for thanks - giv - ing time.

Music and words used by permission of the Korean Hymnal Committee.
Trans. copyright © 1983 by Hae Jong Kim.

HARVEST AND THANKSGIVING

Korean

Acts 14:17, Psalm 65

66 I Am a Stranger

°LÎU-LŌNG-CHÍA

ESTHER RICE, 1980

I-TO LOH, 1980

1. I am a stran-ger. The land is strange, and all I see;
2. I was a stran-ger. The coun-try is fa-mil-iar now;
3. I was a stran-ger. I knew not of the love of God;

The lan-guage is to me just sound. They come and
The words you say I un-der-stand. The crowd a-
My life was filled with hate and fear. I scarce dared

go — the peo-ple 'round. I'm lost. What will the fu-ture be?
round holds out a hand; In thank-ful-ness my head I bow.
to my friend draw near, Un-til your love drew me to God.

I am a stran-ger, a stranger. Who will take me in?
I was a stran-ger, a stranger, and you took me in!
I was a stran-ger, a stranger, but God brought me in.

Music copyright © 1983 by I-to Loh.
Words copyright © 1983 by Esther Rice.

Hebrews 11:13; Ephesians 2:13

CHRISTIAN EXPERIENCE AND DEVOTION

Taiwanese

In Great Thanksgiving

MALATE

67

MELCHIZEDEK M. SOLIS, 1966

MUTYA LOPEZ SOLIS, 1966

1. In great thanks-giv - ing, O Love Di - vine, Who from our sor - row
2. In cel - e - bra - tion of power be-stowed, We who were sin - ners
3. In ded - i - ca - tion we give our lives To heed your bid - ding
4. In ex - al - ta - tion of Christ our Lord, Who for the faith - ful

re - deemed us all, Cleansed of re - gret - ting,
are fol - l'wers bold, For giv - ing en' - mies
to seek the lost, To all the hun - gry
true life en - sured, We laud him Sav - ior,

re - lieved of fear, We come re - joic - ing for new life here.
we sing your praise, With ju - bi - la - tion love's ban-ner raise.
bring food for feasts, To fear-bound peo - ple strength for life's tests.
we teach his way Of peace with jus - tice, hope for to-day.

Romans 12:1

Filipino

CHRISTIAN MISSION AND CONCERN

68   I Raised My Eyes unto the Lord

ŌMIYA

ISAMU MIYAGAWA, 1921
Trans. by VERN ROSSMAN

HATSUE TSUCHIYA, 1930

(♩ = c. 126)

1. I raised my eyes un - to the Lord, Who makes all things new;
2. Je - ru - sa - lem, the beau - ti - ful, De - scend - ed now on me.
3. Oh, hap - py land of light and joy, Where grace shines ev - er bright,
4. How won - der - ful my Sav - ior's love, Wide as the bound-less sea!

The old self died with - in my breast, And fad - ed from my view.
What glo - rious streams of end - less joy Spring up e - ter - na - ly
Dis - pel - ling shad-ows, lift - ing pain, And driv - ing out death's night;
That he should deign to look up - on This poor un - wor - thy me;

This fleet-ing world was lost to sight, My soul trans-formed did see
With - in the hearts of those who live In fel - low-ship with him,
Where, in his warm and ten - der smile, The mel - low fruit hangs rife,
To call me child and make me heir To heav - en's won-drous store,

The new cre - a - tion wrought of God, Light of E - ter - ni - ty.
Whose bless-ings nev - er cease to flow, Whose love can nev - er dim.
In gold - en clus - ters, bend - ing low, Up - on the Tree of Life.
And bid me dwell in halls of peace With him for - ev - er - more.

Words and music used by permission of the Japanese Hymnal Committee.

Revelation 21:1; Isaiah 65:17-19

CHRISTIAN EXPERIENCE AND DEVOTION

Japanese

In Lonely Mountain Ways

GOLDEN HILL*

Sugao Nishimura, 1903
°Trans. by Paul Gregory, 1981

Aaron Chapin, 1805

(♩= c. 120)

1. In lone - ly moun - tain ways Of
2. My jour - ney may be long, The
3. And though when eve - ning falls, A

this world's trial and care, My heart knows naught of
path - way rough and steep; Suf - fi - cient for each
stone my pil - low shapes, The vi - sion of our

fear - scarred days; The Mas - ter's hand is there!
day my song; My way the Lord does keep.
king - dom calls And here a Beth - el makes.

Trans. copyright © 1983 by Paul Gregory.

*This music of Western origin has been accepted as an exception, on the merit of its vivid expression of Japanese sentiment; it is almost regarded as a "Japanese tune."

Psalm 91:11; Genesis 28:10-12

Japanese

MORNING AND EVENING

70 In the Dawn of the Morn

INORI NO ZA

MASUKO ENDO, 1965
°Trans. by NOBUAKI HANAOKA, 1980

TOMOAKI BUNYA, 1965

(♩ = c. 88)

1. In the dawn of the morn, With the dews fresh and
2. In the ray of the sun, On the dyke in the
3. In the dim light of eve, With the feet washed and

clear, I start the new day: With the sick-le held in hand,
field, I lay down my plow; With my hands to-geth-er clasped,
cleansed, I sit on the floor; With the lov-ing fam-i-ly,

I stand on the grass. 'Tis the prayer I pray to
I kneel on the earth. 'Tis the prayer I pray to
Hum-ble meal we share. 'Tis the prayer I pray to

you, "Grate - ful for your day.'"
you, "Grate - ful for your earth."
you, "Grate - ful for your love."

Music and words used by permission of the Japanese Hymnal Committee.
Trans. copyright © 1983 by Nobuaki Hanaoka.

Performance suggestion: #s 4 and 5 on page xii.

Philippians 4:6

MORNING AND EVENING

Japanese

Jesus Christ, Workers' Lord

KEUN-LOH

71

Byung Soo Oh
Trans. by T. Tom Lee
Para. by Elise Shoemaker, 1981

Kook Jin Kim
° Alt., 1981

(♩ = c. 108)

1. Je - sus Christ, work - ers' Lord, We are ser-vants to you.
2. Work - ers we, giv - ing our lives In full serv-ice to you.
3. Roy - al are we, work-ing to serve Je - sus, Sav-ior and King.
4. This lost world, in God's name, We would re-claim in love.

This won-drous world, all of the earth, All cre - a - tion is yours.
With free - dom blessed, un - der your rule, Cit - i - zens all are we.
One fam - i - ly liv - ing in peace Part - ners shar - ing the earth.
New life is brought, mar - vel - ous gift, All in - her - it the earth.

We would work, help - ing to bloom Love - ly flow-ers so rare.
On the fields sow - ing the grain, Har - vest soon we'll reap;
Tools in hand we have reaped Rich har-vest of grains.
Now may we from the dust Fer - tile land re - store,

La - bor and toil, joined with your gifts, Bring fresh fruits of love.
In fac - to - ries, mak - ing the tools, Tools as - sist-ing our need.
By grace of God, we will re - ceive Gifts e - nough for us all.
That there shall come God's par - a - dise, Life from death shall a - rise!

Korean   John 5:17; 9:4   STEWARDSHIP

72 °Lamentation of the Wanderer

°BÊNG SOAN

°After Psalm 137
WU-TUNG HUANG, 1981
Trans. by I-TO LOH, 1981

Based on "Su-Siang-ki" motive
I-TO LOH, 1981

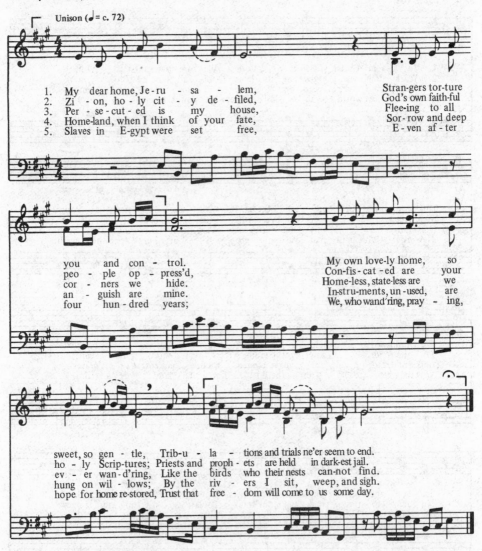

Unison (♩ = c. 72)

1. My dear home, Je-ru-sa-lem,
2. Zi-on, ho-ly cit-y de-filed,
3. Per-se-cut-ed is my house,
4. Home-land, when I think of your fate,
5. Slaves in E-gypt were set free,

Stran-gers tor-ture
God's own faith-ful
Flee-ing to all
Sor-row and deep
E-ven af-ter

you and con-trol.
peo-ple op-press'd,
cor-ners we hide.
an-guish are mine.
four hun-dred years;

My own love-ly home, so
Con-fis-cat-ed are your
Home-less, state-less are we
In-stru-ments, un-used, are
We, who wand'ring, pray-ing,

sweet, so gen-tle, Trib-u-la-tions and trials ne'er seem to end.
ho-ly Scrip-tures; Priests and proph-ets are held in dark-est jail.
ev-er wan-d'ring, Like the birds who their nests can-not find.
hung on wil-lows; By the riv-ers I sit, weep, and sigh.
hope for home re-stored, Trust that free-dom will come to us some day.

Performance suggestion: See #s 1 and 3 on page xii.

JUSTICE AND HUMAN RIGHTS

Taiwanese

Let Us Come unto the Lord

73

PIT

KYUNG LIM OH
°Trans. by T. TOM LEE
Vers. by ESTHER RICE; alt. AAH, 1981

SO WOON OH
°Alt., 1981

(♩= c. 104)

1. Let us come un - to the Lord Who for us is Truth and Life;
2. Thirst - ing souls, long - ing for life, Now we call to you, our God,
3. When we meet dark - ness here, Pow'rs that block and bar our way,
4. Lord our God, you are the Light, On this sea of dark - ness, shine;

Thirst - y soul, wa - ter is here, Liv - ing wa - ter, come and drink.
Lord of Light, an - swer our prayer, As on Car - mel send your fire.
Then we pray as we go: "Ho - ly Spir - it, give us light.
Though the waves bil - low and roll, Safe - ly in your arms we rest.

Je - sus' blood sav - ing from sin, On the cross for us was shed;
Lord, as you prom - ised to us, Send the Ho - ly Spir - it down,
On our path, val - ley and hill, Spread forth beau - ty, give us joy."
Mid the storms, give us, O Lord, Hearts of cour - age trust - ing you.

To the world loud - ly we tell Of God's bound-less love for us.
Then the Word, o'er all the earth, To each cor - ner we will spread.
Then may we, as salt and light, Wit - ness to the world for God.
May we stand, stead-fast in faith, Un - a - shamed be - fore the Lord.

John 14:6

Korean

CHRISTIAN EXPERIENCE AND DEVOTION

74 Light of the World, Salt of the Earth

SU-KONG-PAN

JOHN JYIGIOKK TI'N, 1968
Para. by ERIK ROUTLEY

I-TO LOH, 1968

1. "Light and salt" you called your friends, "On the hill your
2. Each in his own place re - ceives Gos - pel, guid - ance,
3. Men dis - pute and na - tions fight Each all vir - tue

cit - y: Let your light shine out for men,
du - ty: Dai - ly bread and dai - ly work,
claim - ing; Your dis - ci - ple errs and falls,

Music copyright © 1968, 1983 by I-to Loh.
Words copyright © 1968 by John Jyigiokk-Ti'n.
Paraphrase copyright by Agape, Carol Stream, IL 60187. Used by permission.

Performance suggestion: See #s 1 and 3 on page xii.

DAILY LIFE

Taiwanese

Skill and peace and pit - y." But if salt has
Toward the king - dom's beau - ty. Yet the world's dis -
False o - pin - ion fram - ing. Judge me, Lord, and

lost its taste, And the light its fu - el,
tract - ing scene Mocks our loft - y vi - sion.
plead my cause, Light and truth now send me;

And the cit - y shuts its gates, Whence can come re - new - al?
Life's com - plex - i - ties con-fuse Con-science and de - ci - sion.
Lead me in your righ - teous-ness Chas-ten and be - friend me.

Matthew 5:13-16

75 Living in Christ with People

°TONDO

RON O'GRADY, 1980

I-TO LOH, 1980
Motive from Balinese Song, "Meon Meon"

1. Je - sus the Lord stands with the poor,
2. Je - sus the vic - tim, loves the op-pressed.
3. Je - sus the beg - gar lives in the slum,
4. Come to us, Je - sus, strength - en our wills,

When they are hun - gry, he is not fed.
One with the pris - 'ner, locked in a cell,
Seek - ing com - pas - sion, hop-ing for grace,
Bind us to fight a - gainst bond-age and greed,

When they have thirst, he will not drink,
One with the out - cast, one with the slave,
Suf - f'ring in - sults, look-ing for work,
Draw us to share with those who are weak,

Music copyright © 1983 by I-to Loh.
Words copyright © 1983 by Ron O'Grady.

Performance suggestion. Intended for Indonesian bonang (kettle gongs) and saron (metalophone) accompaniment, but keyboard instrument may be used instead. The bonang part usually anticipates the melody.

JUSTICE AND HUMAN RIGHTS

Taiwanese

His   too   the   ag - o - ny   when   they   are   bled.
Bear - ing   the   an - guish   of   each   hu - man   hell.
All   the   world's   ag - o - ny,   etched   on   his   face.
Liv - ing   with   peo - ple   in   ev - 'ry   deed.

Matthew 25:35-40

°The World Is in a Sorry State   76

°TÂI-TANG

ESTHER RICE, 1980
Unison (♩ = c. 76)

Taiwanese folksong, "Tâi-tang tiâu"
Adapt. by I-TO LOH, 1980

1. The world is in a sor - ry state; One's hand a - gainst a
2. The na - tions fight with - out, with - in; Your peo - ple suf - fer
3. O Lord, look down this sor - ry day; Your mer - cy send forth

neigh - bor raised. What then will be your
for their faith. O Lord, we must be
like a stream, That hate and fear may

peo - ple's fate, Lord God, to whom we dai - ly pray?
saved from sin, That all the world may live in love.
wash a - way; And peace a - bound as we have dreamed.

Music adapt. copyright © 1983 by I-to Loh.
Words copyright © 1983 by Esther Rice.
Performance suggestions: See #s 1 and 3 on page xii. No harmony to be added.
Ephesians 5:15; 6:13

Taiwanese

JUSTICE AND HUMAN RIGHTS

77

Living with the Lord

SANG-MYOUNG

Ho Woon Lee, 1967
° Trans. by Hae Jong Kim, 1980

Tae Joon Park, 1967

(♩ = c. 108)

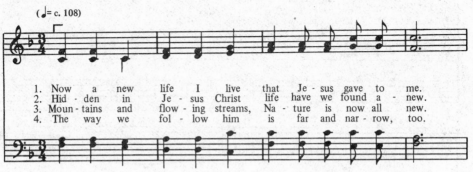

1. Now a new life I live that Je - sus gave to me.
2. Hid - den in Je - sus Christ life have we found a - new.
3. Moun - tains and flow - ing streams, Na - ture is now all new.
4. The way we fol - low him is far and nar - row, too.

Ev - 'ry - thing now is new, Old things have pass'd a - way.
Things I en - joyed be - fore no long - er do I love.
Sin - ners and en - e - mies have all be - come my friends.
Prais - ing him joy - ful - ly, I'll fol - low still the Lord.

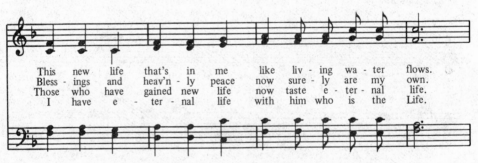

This new life that's in me like liv - ing wa - ter flows.
Bless - ings and heav'n - ly peace now sure - ly are my own.
Those who have gained new life now taste e - ter - nal life.
I have e - ter - nal life with him who is the Life.

Music and words used by permission of the Korean Hymnal Committee.
Trans. copyright © 1983 by Hae Jong Kim.

CHRISTIAN EXPERIENCE AND DEVOTION

Korean

Like rays of bright sun - shine, his love with - in me glows.
Sing - ing praise, breath - ing prayer, I shall live with my Lord.
Here the new heav'n be - gins in my heart with the Lord.
Day by day serv - ing him, I shall live with the Lord.

Refrain

We taste e - ter - nal life; We're liv - ing in the Lord.

Now and for - ev - er we'll be liv - ing in the Lord.

II Corinthians 5:17

78 Loud Our Neighbors' Call Is Heard

YIN CH'IU

T. Z. Koo's *Association Hymnal*
Trans. by MILDRED A. WIANT, c. 1966

Chinese folksong
Arr. by BLISS WIANT, 1934

1. Loud our neigh-bors' call is heard; Chris-tians, rise, pro - claim the word!
2. Quick - ly spread the Chris - tian word, Till our neigh-bors all have heard.

All the na - tions wait to know; God will guide you. For - ward go!
Love up - on the cross com - mands, Rid your soul of pride's de - mands.

Au - tumn fields with gold grain stand, Har - vest time is now at hand,
Change arms in - to use - ful good, Make the world one neigh-bor - hood.

La - bor hard to save the grain, Bind it all for heav - en's gain.
Let us see the hu - man race, Cleansed by God's su - per - nal grace.

Words and music from *Hymns of Universal Praise*, revised edition. Copyright © 1977 by the Chinese Christian Literature Council Ltd., Hong Kong.

Acts 16:9; Matthew 28:18-20

CHRISTIAN MISSION AND CONCERN

Chinese

Love Was Shown upon the Cross 79

CHOONG-SUNG

HEE RO KWON
°Trans. by T. TOM LEE
Vers. by ESTHER RICE; alt. AAH, 1981

CHUNG SOO KIM
°Alt., 1981

1. Love was shown up - on the cross, Where Christ died for me.
2. Still my plea - sure - lov - ing heart Some - times blocks the path.
3. All my world - ly friends are gone, Leav - ing me a - lone.
4. Now as sol - diers of the cross, Fol - low - ing the Lord,

Once I roamed with - out that love, Know - ing not the Lord.
There are those I can - not trust, False and dark their way.
Heav'n - ly love has drawn me close, Wel - come in God's home.
We will find through Word and prayer Christ's own ar - mor strong.

Then I heard Christ clear - ly call, "Come, walk in my way."
Yet I am joy - ful, mind and soul; Christ my jour - ney shares.
Trou - bles, hard - ship come my way; Still I fol - low Christ,
We from temp - ta - tions turn a - side, Seek - ing first the Lord.

Know - ing I be - long to God, Loy - al I would be.
Know - ing I be - long to God, Loy - al I would be.
Know - ing I be - long to God, Loy - al I would be.
Know - ing we be - long to God, Loy - al we shall be.

Music and words used by permission of the Korean Hymnal Committee.
Trans. copyright © 1983 by T. Tom Lee.
Vers. copyright © 1983 by Abingdon Press.

I Corinthians 1:18

Korean

LOVE AND REPENTANCE

80 Now the Day Is Ending

MONING

Elena Maquiso, 1970, Philippines
Trans. by Cirilo Rigos
and Ellsworth Chandlee, 1981

Elena Maquiso, 1970
Philippines

(♩ = c. 112)

1. Now the day is end-ing, Dark-ness is des-cend-ing,
2. In our work and liv-ing, In this day now end-ing,
3. If by be-ing care-less, We have hurt our neigh-bors,
4. If we failed to help the one who need-ed com-fort,
5. Thanks to you, Lord bless-ed, For the day that's end-ed.

Now the birds re-turn-ing, Seek their nest's pro-tec-tion.
Your name have we hal-lowed, Your will have we fol-lowed?
Lord, we ask for mer-cy, Par-don our of-fen-ses.
Or cruel words have spo-ken, Words that hurt and wound-ed.
Cov-er our short-com-ings With your love for-giv-ing

All our work is fin-ished, Time of rest has come.
If to-day we failed you, Lord, for-give, we pray.
Grant to us, O dear Lord, Rec-on-cil-ing love,
Grant us, Lord, your par-don. May we not for-get,
And with rest re-fresh us; Grant a night of peace.

Now for your care this day, Lord, we give you thanks.
Bless with peace our sleep-ing; Be our guard and stay.
that at one we may be As we take our rest.
what you have com-mand-ed, To love one and all.
May we rise to-mor-row, strength-ened and re-newed. A - men.

Psalm 63:5-8

MORNING AND EVENING

Filipino

Praise Our God Above

HSUAN P'ING

81

Tzu-chen Chao, 1931
Trans. by Frank W. Price, 1953

Confucian chant
Harm. by W. H. Wong, 1973
Alt., 1981

Unison (♩ = c. 69)

1. Praise our God a-bove For such bound-less love:
2. God's care like a cloak Wraps us coun-try folk.

Spring wind, sum — mer rain, Then the har — vest grain;
It makes green things grow, Rip — ens what we sow.

Pearl — y rice and corn, Fra — grant au — tumn morn.
Through God we are strong; Sing our har — vest song.

Though our work is hard, God gives us re-ward.
Sing praise, field and flower, Praise gives such might — y power.

Words and music from *Hymns of Universal Praise*, revised edition. Copyright © 1977 by the Chinese Christian Literature Council Ltd., Hong Kong.

Acts 14:17

Chinese

HARVEST AND THANKSGIVING

82 Once to Every Man and Nation

°TYZEN

James Russell Lowell, 1845

Tyzen Hsiao, 1980

(♩ = c. 100)

1. Once to ev – 'ry man and na – tion Comes the
2. Then to side with truth is no – ble, When we
3. By the light of burn – ing mar – tyrs, Christ, your
4. Though the cause of e – vil pros – per, Yet 'tis

mo – ment to de – cide, In the strife of truth with
share her wretch – ed crust, Ere her cause bring fame and
bleed – ing feet we track, Toil – ing up new Cal – v'ries
truth a – lone is strong; Though her por – tion be the

false – hood, For the good or e – vil side; Some great
prof – it, And 'tis pros – p'rous to be just; Then it
ev – er With the cross that turns not back; New oc –
scaf – fold, And up – on the throne be wrong: Yet that

Music copyright © 1983 by Tyzen Hsiao.
JUSTICE AND HUMAN RIGHTS

Taiwanese

cause, God's new Mes — si — ah,
is the brave one choos — es
ca — sions teach new du — ties,
scaf — fold sways the fu — ture,

Of — f'ring each the bloom or blight, And the choice goes by for-
While the cow — ard stands a - side, Till the mul — ti -tude make
Time makes an - cient good un-couth; They must up — ward still and
And, be — hind the dim un-known, Stand-eth God with-in the

rit.

ev — er Twixt that dark — ness and that light.
vir — tue Of the faith they had de — nied.
on — ward, Who would keep a - breast of truth.
shad — ow Keep — ing watch a - bove his own.

rit.

Romans 8:37

83 Our Parting Blest by Christian Bonds

YANG-KUAN SAN-TIEH

Ernest Y. L. Yang, 1933
Trans. by Frank W. Price and Mildred Wiant
Alt. by T. K. Chiu, 1976

Ancient Chinese ch'in melody
Arr. by Tyzen Hsiao, 1981

(♩ = c. 80)

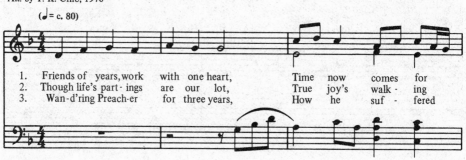

1. Friends of years, work with one heart, Time now comes for
2. Though life's part-ings are our lot, True joy's walk-ing
3. Wan-d'ring Preach-er for three years, How he suf-fered

us to part, Know-ing not when we'll
with our God; When our souls are
with-out fears, Serv-ing oth-ers God's

meet a - gain, These last hours, how sweet with pain!
in God's care, Life can't be a lone - ly 'fair.
will ful-filled, Full of grace and truth re - vealed!

Words and music from *Hymns of Universal Praise*, revised edition. Copyright © 1977 by the Chinese Christian Literature Council Ltd., Hong Kong.
Arr. copyright © 1983 by Tyzen Hsiao.
Text alt. copyright © 1983 by T. K. Chiu.

CHRISTIAN EXPERIENCE AND DEVOTION

Chinese

Refrain

May our gra-cious Lord lead on, guide on! Pass

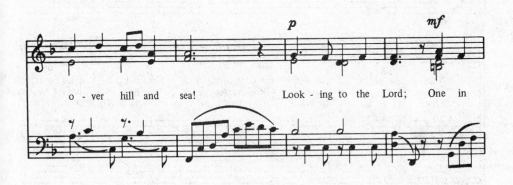

o - ver hill and sea! Look - ing to the Lord; One in

faith, One in hope, Bind our hearts with love in you.

Exodus 40:34-38; Psalm 63:7-8

84 O You Fertile Soil

KUROTSUCHI

Toyohiko Kagawa, 1953
Trans. by Esther Hibbard, 1963

Japanese Gagaku mode
Kazu Nakaseko, 1963

1. O you fer - tile soil, O fer - tile soil, wear - ing your robe
2. Come, O peo - ple of God, a - rise, a - rise, join hands now with
3. Bound-less grace of God! Though oft we stum-ble, we stum-ble and

of rich green, Nur - ture the youths, The youths who tend herds.
true cour - age, Guard your homes, And help the poor,
we fall, God's faith - ful love Will ne'er de - sert us,

In this land of the sun - rise, This land of the sun - rise.
Yea, pro - tect the weak from harm, Pro - tect the weak from harm.
But will strength-en and sus - tain, Will strength-en and sus - tain.

Words used by permission of the Japanese Hymnal Committee and Sumimoto Kagawa.
Music ued by permission of Kiyoaku Sumiya.
Performance suggestion: See #s 1 and 4 on page xii.
STEWARDSHIP

Japanese

Refrain

Sunk in deep need, Rouse this land, O rouse you this land, This land of ours! O God of boun-teous love, O God of boun-teous love, Be with us for-ev-er-more!

Psalms 144:12-15; 82:3,4; 85:10-12

85 Rise Up! All You Slaves of Evil

CH'I-LAI

Pin Wu, 1929
Trans. by Frank W. Price, 1953
Alt., 1981

Ernest Y. L. Yang, 1930
°Harm. by Pen-li Chen, 1981

(♩ = c. 92)

1. Rise up! All you slaves of e - vil, Sin too long has op -
2. Rise up! All you slaves of e - vil, Night too long has con -
3. Rise up! All you slaves of e - vil, Break the chain Sa - tan
4. Rise up! All you slaves of e - vil, Christ has bro - ken the
5. Rise up! All you slaves of e - vil, Fol - low Christ as your

pressed and en - chained you. See now! Christ, the world's
cealed and de - ceived you. See now! Christ, the world's
made to de - stroy you. See now! Christ, the Life e -
dark - est cur - tain. See now! Christ a - lone the
Mas - ter and best Friend. See now! His great king-dom

Sa - vior, He can free you and your strength re - new.
true Light, Your eyes he can with new sight en - due.
ter - nal, He can give life and your free-dom too.
Great Way: Christ your true com-mon - wealth makes cer - tain.
com - ing, Praise to Christ al - ways, world with - out end.

CHRISTIAN MISSION AND CONCERN

Chinese

Rise up! Rise up! All you

slaves of e - vil! Rise up! Be free! For -

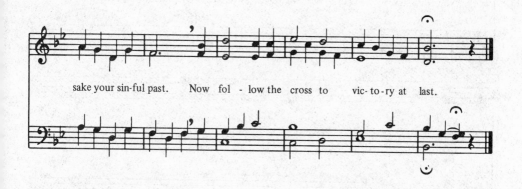

sake your sin-ful past. Now fol - low the cross to vic-to-ry at last.

Romans 13:11-14

86 Shepherds, Awake

KYOUNG-SUNG

JAE BONG PARK
°Trans. by T. TOM LEE, 1981
°Vers. by ESTHER RICE; alt. AAH, 1981

SOO CHUL CHANG
°Alt., 1981

(♩ = c. 116)

1. Shep - herds, a - wake, shep - herds, a - wake From your deep - est sleep.
2. Sun - light of morn spreads o'er the sky, Light - ing earth be - low.
3. Feet grow - ing sore on moun - tain roads, As you lead your sheep;
4. All that you need, cloth - ing e - nough, Shall be yours to wear.

Dark - ness is past, gone is the night, Day - break is com - ing soon.
Green are the hills; Dew on the grass Shines in the gold - en glow.
Breath com - ing short, on hills so steep, The path is of - ten hard.
Rod shall pro - tect you from ev - 'ry harm, Just hold and car - ry it.

And the ho - ri - zon we will see Clear - ly as at noon.
Pas - tures so fresh, ho - ly they seem As the day be - gins.
Yet you shall go, do - ing your task, Ev - 'ry sheep you guard.
"No fears have I, wor - ries are past, For my needs are few.

Shep - herds, a - rise, wake to the dawn, You must tend your sheep.
Shep - herds go forth, lead - ing your flocks, Where green pas - tures grow.
All shep - herds know, du - ty for you, Is the flock to keep.
Now I shall feed all of my sheep In green pas - tures fair."

Psalm 23; Romans 13:11

CHRISTIAN MISSION AND CONCERN   *Korean*

Serving God with Single Heart 87

SHANG SHOU

Ernest Y. L. Yang, 1933
Trans. by Ivy Balchin, 1976

Chia-jen Yang, 1934
Alt., 1981

(♩ = c. 92)

1. Serv - ing God with sin - gle heart, Run the heav'n - ly road with might:
2. God's grace ev - er helped us all O - ver come per - plex - i - ty;
3. God's grace flows a - bun - dant - ly, Giv - ing health and pur - i - ty;
4. Hon - or age with man - y friends, Thank - ing God with prayer and praise;

In God's ho - ly work en - gage, Lead - ing all to live a - right.
Cheer - ful - ly the cross we bear; Faith and love grow con - stant - ly.
Peace of heart yields hap - pi - ness, Crowned with rare lon - gev - i - ty.
Life, then, like a loft - y tree, Bear - ing ben - e - fi - cial days.

Refrain

Our re - spect to age we pay, God's grace grows from day to day.

Words and music from *Hymns of Universal Praise*, revised edition. Copyright © 1977 by the Chinese Christian Literature Council Ltd., Hong Kong.

Philippians 2:13-14

Chinese

CHRISTIAN FAMILY

88   The Call for Reapers

CHOO-SOO

J. O. THOMPSON, 1885

WOON YOUNG RA

1. Far and near the fields are teem-ing   With the waves of rip - ened
2. Send them forth with morn's first beam-ing,   Send them in the noon - tide's
3. O you whom the Lord is send-ing,   Gath - er now the sheaves of

Changgo
(drum)

grain;   Far and near their gold is gleam-ing
glare;   When the sun's last ray's are gleam-ing,
gold;   Heav'n-ward then at eve - ning wend-ing,

Music and words used by permission of the Korean Hymnal Committee.

Performance suggestions: See # 6 on page xii.

STEWARDSHIP

Korean

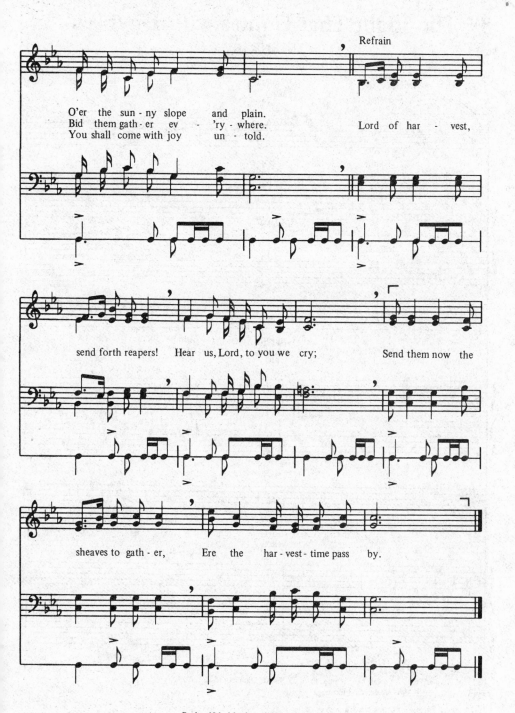

O'er the sun - ny slope and plain.
Bid them gath - er ev - 'ry - where.
You shall come with joy un - told.

Refrain

Lord of har - vest, send forth reapers! Hear us, Lord, to you we cry; Send them now the sheaves to gath - er, Ere the har - vest - time pass by.

Psalm 126; Matthew 9:37; John 9:4

89 The Light That Comes with Daybreak

ETENRAKU

TOMOTSUNE YANAGIDA, 1966
°Trans. by SANDY FUKUNAGA, 1980

Gagaku melody
Arr. by HIKARU HAYASHI, 1967

1. The light that comes with day break,
   eve - ning lit by moon, Sum - mers filled with
   flow'rs, win - ter's trees all cov - ered with

2. Strength dur - ing times of sor - row,
   com - fort and hope are giv'n; Trust in the Lord's un-
   chang - ing our love and guid - ing to

3. Days may all pass so quick - ly,
   time es - capes us all; Love and beau - ty
   fill our hearts in praise to

Performance suggestions: See #s 2 and 5 on page xii.

MORNING AND EVENING

Japanese

snow. Each day's joys are shared with each
hand. Shar - ing grief to - geth - er can
God. Each day's joys are shared with each

oth - er and the Lord, sun - light and
make us strong - er in love; we weath - er the
oth - er and the Lord; for all your

beau - ty sur - round us, we thank you, God.
bur - den of all grief but lean on God.
gifts of light and life, we thank you, God.

Psalms 127; 128

90 The Sun of Righteousness

GI NO TAIYŌ

Kō Yūki, 1923
°Trans. by June Nakada Sumida, 1981

Ugo Nakada, 1930

(♩ = c. 96)

1. Lo, the Sun of righ-teous-ness, Breaks forth in-to Light;
2. Gone is now the twi-light deep, Swift it's dark re-treat;
3. In the bright-ness of the Light, Dim is earth-ly gain;
4. Let the flame of ho-li-ness, Fire of love di-vine,

From th'ho-ri-zon of the soul, Ban-ished is the night.
Pierc-ing through the earth and sky, Where the heav-ens meet,
Tem-po-ral is mor-tal fame; Fleet-ing, pow'r and pain.
Burn the dross, re-new-al bring, Cleanse this life of mine.

In the bounds of fi-nite strength, We our lim-its faced,
Break-ing forth with thun-d'rous voice, Light now o-ver-flows!
Oh, the pov-er-ty of soul— Flee-ing from God's face,
Let the Sun of righ-teous-ness Glow in might-y pow'r;

Si-lent-ly, in glo-rious pow'r, God, our world, has graced.
Bathed in rays of righ-teous-ness, All cre-a-tion glows.
On-ly to re-turn and find Par-don-ing grace.
Let it light my path of faith, Ev-'ry day and hour.

Words and music used by permission of the Japanese Hymnal Committee.
Trans. copyright © 1983 by June Nakada Sumida.

John 1:9

CHRISTIAN EXPERIENCE AND DEVOTION

Japanese

To the One Creator of All

HUN-SHIN

91

Won Yong Ra
°Trans. by T. Tom Lee
Para. by Elise Shoemaker, 1981

Woon Young Ra

(♩. = c. 80)

1. To the One Cre - a - tor of all, In whose like-ness we are made,
2. From the pow'r of death and sin, God's sal - va - tion sets us free;
3. Un - der shelt - 'ring love of God, Each new day rich mer - cy be - stows;

Hymns of thanks we ded - i - cate, Prais - es to our gra - cious God.
Hymns of thanks we ded - i - cate, Prais - es to our gra - cious God.
Hymns of thanks we ded - i - cate, Prais - es to our gra - cious God.

Refrain

We would bring these gifts to you, all our lives as of - f'ring to you.

Thanks we sing, gifts we bring, Now ac - cept our of - fer - ing.

Music and words used by permission of the Korean Hymnal Committee.
Trans. copyright © 1983 by T. Tom Lee.
Para. copyright © 1983 by Abingdon Press.   *Genesis 1:27*
Korean

STEWARDSHIP

92 To the Yearly Seasons

NANKING

ERNEST Y. L. YANG, 1934
Trans. by IVY BALCHIN, 1973

S. A. CHIU WOO, 1935
°Harm. by TYZEN HSIAO, 1981

1. To the year-ly sea - sons   Spring-time gives the birth:
2. Hu-man-kind God cares   for,   As the source of all:
3. Hu-man-kind God trea - sures: Boun-teous grace he gave;
4. Saints and sa-ges ev - er   God's great Word made known:

Reds and crim-sons, grass-es fra-grant, gild the earth.
God cre - ates my earth-ly bod - y, and my soul:
In the Son was God made flesh the world to save.
Through the a - ges peo-ple praise the fil - ial child.

Na - ture in its beau - ty   Sings God's gra-cious-ness,
Still God guides as ev - er: In the Book I see
See his gen - tle child - hood,   What a pat-tern fair,
I would learn this vir - tue,   And God's law re - vere,

CHRISTIAN FAMILY

Chinese

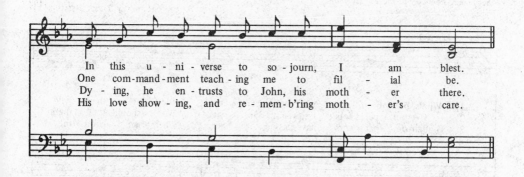

In this u - ni - verse to so - journ, I am blest.
One com - mand - ment teach - ing me to fil - ial be.
Dy - ing, he en - trusts to John, his moth - er there.
His love show - ing, and re - mem - b'ring moth - er's care.

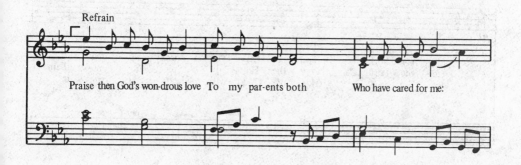

Refrain

Praise then God's won-drous love To my par-ents both Who have cared for me:

Hu-man-kind's sal - va - tion free Is our song e - ter - nal - ly.

Exodus 20:12; Ephesians 6:1-3

93 Who's Been Born Without Two Parents?

FILIAL PIETY

Anonymous, from *Nevius-Mateer Hymnal*
Trans. by MILDRED A. WIANT

RUTH STAHL, 1934
°Harm. by TYZEN HSIAO, 1981

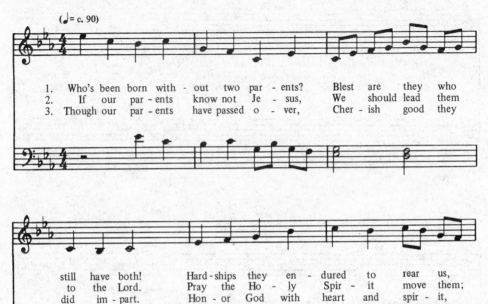

(♩ = c. 90)

1. Who's been born with - out two par - ents? Blest are they who
2. If our par - ents know not Je - sus, We should lead them
3. Though our par - ents have passed o - ver, Cher - ish good they

still have both! Hard - ships they en - dured to rear us,
to the Lord. Pray the Ho - ly Spir - it move them;
did im - part. Hon - or God with heart and spir - it,

How dare we for - get their worth?
Hap - py fam - i - lies serve one God.
Till we're joined, no more to part.

CHRISTIAN FAMILY

Chinese

Refrain

Hon - or par - ents, fil - ial be; God's com - mand we must o - bey.

Fol - l'wing the di - vine de - cree, Homes will all much hap - pier be.

Exodus 20:12; Luke 2:51

94 Vast Throngs in the Stark Wilderness

KUEI CHEN

Feng-yüan Chang, c. 1907
Trans. by Mildred A. Wiant, c. 1966
Alt., 1981

Pao-chen Li, 1934
Harm. by W. H. Wong, 1969

(♩ = c. 80)

1. Vast throngs in the stark wil - der - ness,
2. The path a - head is dark - er yet,
3. At last heav - en's true light de - scends,
4. Re - joice to see heav - en's throng,
5. Once know - ing not the joy of lov - ing care,

Their days spend con - fused and lost,
Where Sa - tan now is the guide,
To flood the mis - lead - ing path;
Quick beck - 'ning to en - ter in.
Feel - ing lost and wan - d'ring in de - spair,

Long part - ed from hap - pi - ness.
Di - rect - ing to a great a - byss.
Then quick - ly one com - pre - hends,
If you would es - cape from wrong,
Find - ing now the love God has long wished to share,

They know no kind lov - ing care.
Where can a safe way be found?
The past has been veiled in sin.
Now come to God's sus - tain - ing arms.
What joy reigns in heav - en now!

Exodus 13:21-22; 14:10-13; 18:10-12

CHRISTIAN EXPERIENCE AND DEVOTION

Chinese

Your Kingdom Come

LÂM SÎN

Japanese: Kō Yŭki, 1929
Taiwanese: John Jyigiokk Ti'n, alt., 1980
Trans. by I-to Loh, 1980

I-to Loh, 1980

(♩ = c. 88)

1. On the shore of Gal - i - lee, Branch-es wav - ing in the breeze,
2. Through the days of pain and trial, And the nights of fear - ful cries,
3. Lord, when will you hear our prayers, Bring your king-dom down to earth?

There Lord Je - sus preached good news That God's king-dom now is near.
Christ our Sav - ior's ev - er near; He shall o - ver - come our fears.
When shall op-pres - sion, hate dis-ap- pear, Peace and love for - ev-er pre-vail?

Refrain

Though two thou-sand years have passed, Still we pray, "Your kingdom come.

May your will be done on earth, As it is in heav-en."

Music and trans. copyright © 1983 by I-to Loh.
Japanese words copyright by the Japanese Hymnal Committee.
Taiwanese words copyright © 1983 by John Jyigiokk Ti'n.

Matthew 6:9-10; Mark 1:15

Taiwanese

JUSTICE AND HUMAN RIGHTS

IV
Children

Dear Lord, Lead Me Day by Day   96

COTTAGE GROVE

FRANCISCA ASUNCION, 1976

Philippine folk melody
Adapt. by FRANCISCA ASUNCION, 1976

(♩ = c. 80)

1. Dear Lord, lead me day by day; Make me stead-fast, wise, and strong.
2. Dear Lord, lead me day by day; Make me fol - low and o - bey
3. Now with con - fi-dence I sing Joy-ous prais - es to our King,

Hap - py most of all to know That my dear Lord loves me so.
Faith - ful - ly your words of life, That your love ev - er a - bide.
And with up - right heart I give ten - der care and sym - pa - thy.

Refrain

Praise to God, Fount of love, Praise from morn till the set of sun.

Praise at home, praise in Church; Praise to God ev - 'ry where on earth.

Psalm 23:3

Filipino

CHILDREN

97 Gentle Jesus, Meek and Mild

SINIM

Charles Wesley, 1767

Chinese folksong
Harm. W. H. Wong, 1976

(♩= c. 92)

1. Gen - tle Je - sus, meek and mild, Look up - on a
2. Lamb of God, I look to thee; Thou shalt my ex -
3. Fain I would be as thou art; Give me thy o -
4. Lov - ing Je - sus, gen - tle Lamb, In thy gra - cious

lit - tle child; Pit - y my sim - plic - i - ty;
am - ple be; Thou art gen - tle, meek, and mild;
be - dient heart. Thou art pit - i - ful and kind;
hands I am; Make me, Sav - ior, what thou art;

Suf - fer me to come to thee.
Thou wast once a lit - tle child.
Let me have thy lov - ing mind.
Live thy - self with - in my heart. A - men.

Music from *Hymns of Universal Praise*, revised edition. Copyright © 1977 by the Chinese Christian Literature Council Ltd., Hong Kong.

II Corinthians 8:9

CHILDREN

Chinese

Jesus Loved Each Little Child
CECILIA

Tzu-chen Chao
Trans. by Frank W. Price, 1953

Chinese folksong
Harm. by Bliss Wiant, 1934

1. Je - sus loved each lit - tle child, On all chil - dren Je - sus smiled, Oth - ers shout - ed, "Go a - way." Je - sus said, "Come un - to me!"
2. Gen - tle Je - sus, good and kind, Praised the hum - ble child - like mind; All who in his love be - lieve His dear bless - ing may re - ceive.
3. Je - sus loves each lit - tle child; Chil - dren love the Sav - ior mild. Bring the chil - dren to his arms; They shall be safe from all that harms.
4. Each child with a glad, pure heart In his king - dom has a part. All with child - like faith and grace In his king - dom have a place.

Words and music from *Hymns of Universal Praise*, revised edition. Copyright © 1977 by the Chinese Christian Literature Council Ltd., Hong Kong.

Mark 10:13-16

Chinese

CHILDREN

99 Joyful Christmas Day Is Here

KURISUMASU

Toshiaki Okamoto
°Trans. by Hidemi Itō and Sandra Fukunaga, 1981

Toshiaki Okamoto

(♩ = c. 88)

Round *I *f*   *II

1. Joy - ful, joy - ful, joy - ful, joy - ful, Christ-mas day is here;
2. Joy - ful, hap - py, joy - ful, hap - py, Christ-mas day is here;
(optional) 3. Hap - py, hap - py, hap - py, hap - py, Christ-mas day is here;

mf

Ding, ding, dong, dong, Hear the church bells ring.
Ding, ding, dong, dong, Christ - mas day is here.
Jing, jing, cling, cling, Hear the sleigh bells ring.

mf

Words and music by Toshiaki Okamoto, used by permission of JASRAC, license no. 8211927.
Trans. copyright © 1983 by Hidemi Ito and Sandra Fukunaga.
*Performance suggestion: Can be sung as a round, 2nd voice starts one measure after.

CHILDREN

Japanese

Chime through-out the land, He was born in Beth - le - hem;
Chime through-out the land, He was born in Beth - le - hem;
San - ta Claus will come with his sleigh all filled with toys;

Ba - by Je - sus came in - to this world on Christ - mas day.
Ba - by Je - sus came in - to this world on Christ - mas day.
Gifts and good news he will bring to chil - dren of the world.

Hap - py, hap - py, hap - py, hap - py, Christ - mas day is here;
Sing to - geth - er, cel - e - brate Je - sus' birth - day;
Hap - py, hap - py, hap - py, hap - py, Christ - mas day is here;

Ding, ding, dong, dong, Hear the church bells ring.
Ding, ding, dong, dong, Christ-mas day is here.
Jing, jing, cling, cling, Hear the sleigh bells ring.

Luke 2:8-14

100 Jesus Merciful

TZU-CHEN CHAO, 1931
Trans. by FRANK W. PRICE
Alt. by T. K. Chiu, 1976

HUBBARD

Chinese traditional melody
Arr. by BLISS WIANT, 1934
Alt., 1981

(♩ = c. 88)

1. Je - sus mer - ci - ful, Most friend - ly, most kind,
2. Je - sus brave and bold, Most hum - ble, most wise;
3. Je - sus, gra - cious Lord, Pa - tient and ten - der;
4. Je - sus' love most pure, Most just and most true;

He can change my heart, Give me his own mind.
Comes to walk with me, Saves me, with his life!
Shar - ing all my pain, Bear - ing all my load.
God's rule he ex - tends; New life he cre - ates.

Words and music from *Hymns of Universal Praise*, revised edition. Copyright © 1977 by the Chinese Christian Literature Council Ltd., Hong Kong.
Text alt. copyright © 1983 by T. K. Chiu.
CHILDREN   *Mark 2:13-17; 15:39; Acts 4:10-12*   *Chinese*

101 Jesus My Friend Is Great

KATSUSHIKO SHIMADA
YUJI ABE, 1963
Trans. by NOBUAKI HANAOKA, 1981

KANTŌ

KATSUHIKO SHIMADA
YUJI ABE, 1963

(♩ = c. 104)

F   C   Gm   C   F

1. Je - sus my friend is great; Je - sus my friend is true;
2. Je - sus my Lord is kind; Je - sus my Lord is strong.
3. Je - sus hears my prayers; Je - sus hears my songs.

Am   Dm   Gm   C   F   C7   F

Je - sus my friend is great and true; I am not a - fraid.
Je - sus my Lord is kind and strong; I am not a - fraid.
Je - sus is with you and me; We are not a - fraid.

Music and words copyright © 1983 by Katsuhiko Shimada and Yuji Abe.
Trans. copyright © 1983 by Nobuaki Hanaoka.

John 10:11; Matthew 28:20b

CHILDREN   *Japanese*

°Let Us Even Now Go

MANGLAKAT

102

Stanza 1: trad.
Stanzas 2 & 3 by Lois F. Bello, 1981

Arr. Elena G. Maquiso, 1958

(♩= c. 144)

Bb

1. Let us e - ven now go to Beth - le - hem,
2. Let us e - ven now of - fer love and praise
3. Let us e - ven now sing with heart and soul:

Cm   **F7**   **Bb**

Go to Beth - le - hem of Ju - de - a.
To the Lord our God, to the Lord our God,
"Christ was born to save! Christ was born to save!"

Je - sus Christ our Lord, He is the King of kings;
Who from heav - en's throne has sent a gift of love,
Let us sing our praise that all the world may know,

Cm   **F7**   **Bb**

Now in Beth - le - hem is born!
Je - sus Christ, God's on - ly Son,
All the world may know God's love,

Cm   **F7**   **Bb**

Now in Beth - le - hem is born!
Je - sus Christ, God's on - ly Son.
All the world may know God's love.

Luke 2:15

Filipino

CHILDREN

103 Para Para Pitter Pat

NAKADA

Ugo Nakada
Trans. by June Nakada Sumida, 1981

Harm. by Masao Tomioka

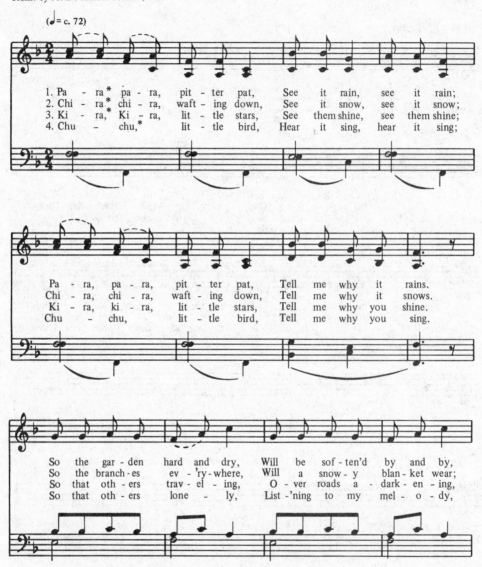

1. Pa - ra* pa - ra, pit - ter pat, See it rain, see it rain;
2. Chi - ra* chi - ra, waft - ing down, See it snow, see it snow;
3. Ki - ra, Ki - ra, lit - tle stars, See them shine, see them shine;
4. Chu - chu,* lit - tle bird, Hear it sing, hear it sing;

Pa - ra, pa - ra, pit - ter pat, Tell me why it rains.
Chi - ra, chi - ra, waft - ing down, Tell me why it snows.
Ki - ra, ki - ra, lit - tle stars, Tell me why you shine.
Chu - chu, lit - tle bird, Tell me why you sing.

So the gar - den hard and dry, Will be sof - ten'd by and by,
So the branch - es ev - 'ry - where, Will a snow - y blan - ket wear;
So that oth - ers trav - el - ing, O - ver roads a - dark - en - ing,
So that oth - ers lone - ly, List - 'ning to my mel - o - dy,

Words by Ugo Nakada and music by Masao Tomioka, used by permission of JASRAC, license no. 8211927.
Trans. copyright © 1983 by June Nakada Sumida.

*representing onomatopoeic expressions in Japanese.

CHILDREN

Japanese

And the flow - ers one by one, Soon will see the sun.
Warm and co - zy they will stay, On a win - ter's day.
Soon will find their path - ways bright, In the star - ry light.
In their hearts will hear me say, "God loves you to - day.

Acts 14:17; Matthew 5:45

°Amen, Praise the Father   104

°HELENA

Leng Loh, 1981   Leng Loh, 1981

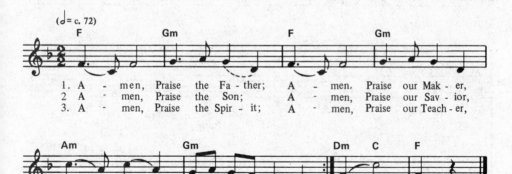

($\quad$ = c. 72)

| F | Gm | F | Gm |

1. A - men, Praise the Fa - ther; A - men, Praise our Mak - er,
2. A - men, Praise the Son; A - men, Praise our Sav - ior,
3. A - men, Praise the Spir - it; A - men, Praise our Teach - er,

| Am | Gm | Dm C F |

A - men, A - men. A - men.

Music and words copyright © 1983 by Leng Loh.

II Corinthians 13:13

Taiwanese   *CHILDREN*

105

°My Creed

°DANIEL BLISS

DANI D. AGUILA, 1981

DANI D. AGUILA, 1981
Harm. by E. D. THOMPSON

1. Learn to live, live to love; Love to laugh, laugh to lilt; Lilt to lift, lift to lead; Lead to learn, learn to live.
2. Let this creed guide me, Lord; Both in deed and in word; Ev - 'ry day let me care, Ev - 'ry way let me share.
3. When at last all is done, And to dust I am gone; From this earth let me part Full of joy in my heart.

I Corinthians 10:31

CHILDREN

Filipino

The Church Stands, Built So Firmly 106

ORINI

CHUNG HOON CHE
°Trans. by T. TOM LEE
Vers. by ESTHER RICE; alt. AAH,1981

CHONG KEUN CHUN

(♩ = c. 108)

1. The church stands, built so firm - ly, on the rock of faith.
2. The church shines, light - ing bright - ly, tell - ing us of hope.
3. The church lifts up to heav - en, as the arms of Christ,

Chil - dren, O lit - tle chil - dren, lift to God your prayers.
Chil - dren, O lit - tle chil - dren, sing your hymns of praise.
Chil - dren, the lit - tle chil - dren, strength-ened in the Word.

Stand - ing be - fore you is the lad - der un - to heav'n.
Sing as the an - gel choirs, who sing in heav'n a - bove.
May God's full truth and light as man - na come to all,

Glo - ry from God a - bove shall Come to you to - day.
Sing of your hope and joy, O sing of God's great love.
Bring - ing a king - dom come to earth through Christ our Lord.

Luke 18:16-17

Korean

CHILDREN

v
Youth

107

A Grain of Wheat

MUGI

Toyohiko Kagawa, composite, 1981
Trans. stanza 1 by Frank Y. Ohtomo, 1981
Trans. stanzas 2, 3 by Jonathan Fujita, 1981

Ushio Takahashi, 1976

1. When a grain of wheat Into the ground
2. Young peo - ple, in your hands, The fu - ture lies
3. For the sake of love, The sake of love

has fall - en, In - to the cold ground,
in your hands, Young peo - ple, in your hands,
of Je - sus, For the sake of love,

And lies in wait - ing for the spring, And lies in
The fu - ture lies in your hands; Take up your
The sake of love of Je - sus, Though walk- ing

Performance suggestion: See #s 4 and 5 on page xii.

YOUTH

Japanese

					F			
wait	-	ing	for	the	spring;	This	fall -	en
cross,		take	up	your	cross;	Live	with	the
through		the	thorn -	y	road,	Though	walk -	ing

					Am			
grain		will	rise	to	life,	This	fall -	en
strength		of	Je -	sus	Christ,	Live	with	the
through		the	thorn -	y	road,	Young	peo -	ple

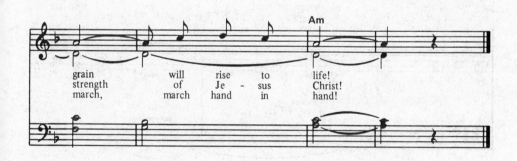

					Am		
grain		will	rise	to	life!		
strength		of	Je -	sus	Christ!		
march,		march	hand	in	hand!		

John 12:24

108 Climb on, Climb on, Young Friend

ASCENDIMUS

Kō Yūki, 1940
Trans. by George Gish, 1980

Yasurō Ishimaru, 1940

(♩ = c. 100)

1. Climb on, climb on, young friend. Fol - low the path-way lead - ing a -
2. Climb on, climb on, with faith. Fol - low the path-way lead - ing a -
3. Help to each oth - er give a - long the path-way lead - ing a -

bove. Al - though the fields be - low with mist are
bove. Al - though the wind and rain with fu - ry
bove. If some-one fall - en be, and strick - en

Words by Kō Yūki, used by permission of JASRAC, license no. 8211927.
Trans. copyright © 1983 by George Gish.

YOUTH

Japanese

shroud-ed, friend, still climb on. High a - bove o'er the
block the way, friend, climb on. Up a - bove the dark
down with pain on the way, Tend with care to their

peaks The sun is shin - ing in splen - dor bright.
clouds The air is clear and the sky is blue.
needs, And com-fort give with the hands of love.

A - long the nar-row way, Keep pressing on, young friend, still climb on.
Have faith in God's great power, And brave-ly trust-ing it, still climb on.
Point-ing to peaks on high, Climb on to-geth - er, friend, still climb on.

Matthew 7:13-14

109 Every Day, Every Hour

LILY CHUNG, 1979

LILY CHUNG, 1979

1. Ev-'ry day and ev-'ry hour, we will walk hand in hand with
2. day and ev-'ry hour, when we shall seek your will in

God; Ev-'ry day and ev-'ry hour, God's love will be with
life; Ev-'ry day and ev-'ry hour, keep us in tune with

us. Ev-'ry time when we doubt, God's hand will
you. Ev-'ry time, if we shall fall, Your grace will

YOUTH

Chinese

guide us through, through each year, through each day; we'll walk hand
be with us, through good times, through bad times; we'll walk hand

1. in hand with God.   Ev-'ry
   in hand with

2.

in hand with God.
in hand with you.

Violin Part

Matthew 18:20; 28:20

110 Regret

George J. Chiu, 1977

George J. Chiu, 1977

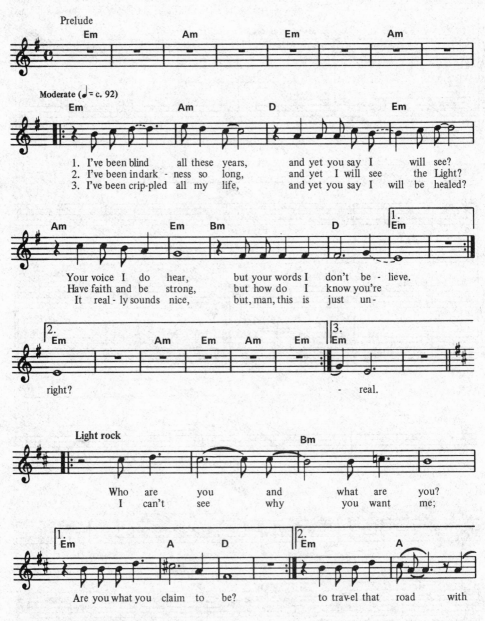

Prelude

Moderate (♩ = c. 92)

1. I've been blind all these years, and yet you say I will see?
2. I've been in dark-ness so long, and yet I will see the Light?
3. I've been crip-pled all my life, and yet you say I will be healed?

Your voice I do hear, but your words I don't be - lieve.
Have faith and be strong, but how do I know you're
It real-ly sounds nice, but, man, this is just un-

right?

- real.

Light rock

Who are you and what are you?
I can't see why you want me;

Are you what you claim to be?

to trav-el that road with

YOUTH

Taiwanese

Dsus D G A 1. Am

you.   What's so great a - bout that gate   that you talk a-bout so
       I can't see and   I   can't walk,

Em 2. Am Em G

much?   I don't need you,   nor your talk.   I don't need a

D G D G

crutch,   I don't need a   crutch.   I don't need a

D Em B E A D

crutch, I don't need a   crutch!

Slower (choppy)
G D Em

Some-times I wish you had   tak-en me by the hands   and
I wish that I knew   what you said was true   and could

Am 1. Am Em 2. Am

forced me,   O forced me to un - der - stand.   come a - long with
come a - long, could

Em Am D

you,   Please help me   to come a - long with   you.

Em Am Em

Oo.

John 9:25

111 °To Jesus, with Love

GEORGE J. CHIU, 1976

GEORGE J. CHIU, 1976

YOUTH

Taiwanese

Revelation 22:20

112 We Need Your Powerful Hand, Dear Lord

HELPING HANDS

Yuri L. Torigoe, 1981

Yuri L. Torigoe, 1981
Alt., AAH, 1981

With spirit (♩.= 76)

1. We need your pow'r-ful hand, dear Lord, we
2. We'll give a help-ing hand, oh, Lord, we'll

need your bless - ing hand   To guide us in our hopes to build a
give a gra - cious hand   To fill our land with joy and peace may

peace - ful, lov - ing   land.   To free the earth from hate and greed and
kind-ness nev - er   cease.   To see your un - i - verse as one we

prej - u - dice we breed.   Give us your pow'r-ful hand, dear lord, Give
share be-neath the sun.   We'll give a help - ing hand, oh, Lord, We'll

Music and words copyright © 1983 by Yuri L. Torigoe.

YOUTH

Japanese

us   your bless-ing   hand.
give   a gra - cious   hand.   In   the hearts both

near and far we'll find a like-ness   there,   Hope and fear and

joy and tears, each must some bur-den   bear.   With love and faith and

trust reach out, God's king-dom we will   share.   God's strength and grace will

D.C. (to Verse 2)

fill   us with one   mind and will   to   care.

Matthew 19:13; Mark 5:23

VI

Psalms and Service Music

°Come, O Gracious King 113

°THEVARAM

D. S. Dharmapalan, 1981

Karnatic melody, Sri Lanka
As sung by D. S. Dharmapalan, 1981
Transcr. by I-to Loh

(♩ = c. 69)

1. Come, O gra - cious King, O come; Let your pres-ence us
2. May your gra - cious-ness at - tend, That our prayers to you

re - fine. Give your bless-ings, Lord, we pray;
as - cend _ Lend your - self to us, we pray;

Ho - ly and Might - y One, O come.
With your mer - cies us ar - ray.

Transcr. copyright © 1983 by I-to Loh.
Words copyright © 1983 by D. S. Dharmapalan.

Performance suggestions: See #1 on page xii. No harmony to be added.

Psalm 24:7-10

Sri Lankan

SERVICE MUSIC

°Jesus' Name Is Our Refuge 114

°SARANAM

Traditional Tamil text
Trans. by D. S. Dharmapalan, 1981

Karnatic melody, Sri Lanka
As sung by D. S. Dharmapalan, 1981
Transcr. by I-to Loh

(♩ = c. 138)

Je - sus' name is our ref - uge; King of kings, his name's our ref - uge.

Om - nip - o - tent, God's name's our ref - uge; Love di-vine, God's name's our ref - uge.

Transcr. copyright © 1983 by I-to Loh.
Trans. copyright © 1983 by D. S. Dharmapalan.

Performance suggestion: No harmony to be added.

Psalm 46; Ephesians 1:21

Sri Lankan

SERVICE MUSIC

115 °Be Gracious to Me, O God

°PÎN-TONG

Based on Psalm 57:1, 7-10
Tsung-hsien Yang, 1980

Tsung-hsien Yang, 1980

Allegretto (♩ = c. 80)

Copyright © 1983 by Tsung-hsien Yang.

Performance suggestions: In unison for congregation. When sung as a canon by the choir, *is the last note for vss. 1 and 2.

Taiwanese

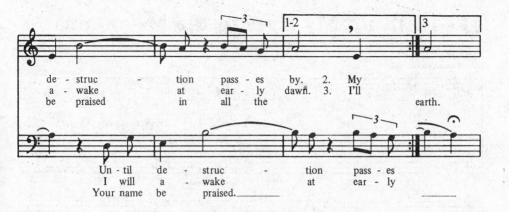

de - struc - tion pass - es by. 2. My
a - wake at ear - ly dawn. 3. I'll
be praised in all the earth.

Un - til de - struc - tion pass - es
I will a - wake at ear - ly
Your name be praised.____

How Blessed Are They 116

ROCKEY

Psalm 32 in Urdu
Trans. by C. D. ROCKEY
Alt., 1981

Pakistani melody
Transcr. by the Rev. and Mrs. P. J. ACTON
Alt., 1981

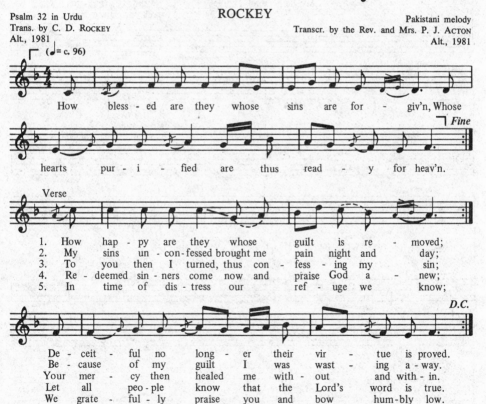

(♩ = c. 96)

How bless - ed are they whose sins are for - giv'n, Whose

Fine

hearts pur - i - fied are thus read - y for heav'n.

Verse

1. How hap - py are they whose guilt is re - moved;
2. My sins un - con - fessed brought me pain night and day;
3. To you then I turned, thus con - fess - ing my sin;
4. Re - deemed sin - ners come now and praise God a - new;
5. In time of dis - tress our ref - uge we know;

D.C.

De - ceit - ful no long - er their vir - tue is proved.
Be - cause of my guilt I was wast - ing a - way.
Your mer - cy then healed me with - out and with - in.
Let all peo - ple know that the Lord's word is true.
We grate - ful - ly praise you and bow hum - bly low.

Music transcr. copyright © 1983 by P. J. Acton.
Trans. copyright © 1983 by Helen C. Rockey. Used by permission.
Performance suggestions: See #6 on page xii. No harmony to be added.

Pakistani

PSALMS

117 I Lift up My Eyes to the Mountains

°TSŬ-CHU-TIAO

Psalm 121 (Grail, alt.)

Chinese folksong, "Tsŭ-chu-tiao"
Adapt. by PEN-LI CHEN, 1980

Unison (♩ = c. 72)

1. I lift up my eyes to the moun-tains: whence shall come my
2. The Lord is your guard and your shade, stand-ing at your right

help? My help shall come from the Lord
side. By day the sun shall not smite you

who made heav - en and earth. May God nev - er
nor the moon in the night. God pro - tects you

let you stum - ble! The pro - tec - tor
from all dan - ger, and guards your soul

of Is - ra - el sleeps not nor slum - bers.
as you come and go now and for - ev - er.

Music adapt. copyright © 1983 by Pen-li Chen.
Psalm 121, from *The Psalms: A New Translation* published by William Collins Sons & Co. Ltd., is reprinted by permission of the Grail, England.

PSALMS

Chinese

May the Lord, Mighty God 118

WEN TI

ANONYMOUS

From PAO-CHEN LI'S "Wen Ti"
Adapt. AAH, 1980

May the Lord, might-y God, Bless and keep you for-

ev - er; Grant you peace, per - fect

peace, Cour - age in ev - 'ry en - deav - or.

Descant (a few female voices)

Lift up and see his face, his grace for-

Melody

Lift up your eyes and see his face, And his grace for-

ev - er; May the Lord, might - y

ev - er; May the Lord, might - y

God, Bless and keep you for - ev - er.

God, Bless and keep you for - ev - er.

Numbers 6:24-26

Chinese

SERVICE MUSIC

119 Longing for the Lord

AHNG-MOH

Based on Psalm 42
YOUNG TACK CHUN
Trans. by T. TOM LEE, 1981
Vers. by ESTHER RICE, 1981

JAE HOON PARK
Alt., 1981

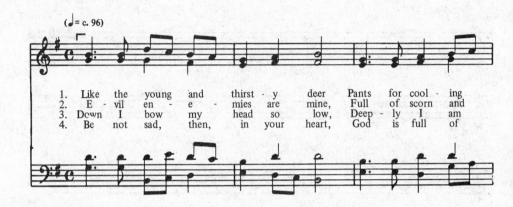

(♩ = c. 96)

1. Like the young and thirst - y deer Pants for cool - ing
2. E - vil en - e - mies are mine, Full of scorn and
3. Down I bow my head so low, Deep - ly I am
4. Be not sad, then, in your heart, God is full of

wa - ter, Strug - gling toward the stream so clear
say - ing, "Where's the God for whom you pine,
sigh - ing, Long - ing for God's house be - low,
kind - ness; Love will shine and ne'er de - part,

Words and music used by permission of the Korean Hymnal Committee.
Trans. copyright © 1983 by T. Tom Lee.
Vers. copyright © 1983 by Esther Rice.

PSALMS

Korean

Where he'll quench his thirst, So my long-ing
Where's the God you seek?" Through long days they
An - cient tem - ple loved. Lord, your wa - ter-
Bright - 'ning all your days. Heav'n - ly songs will

soul de - sires To draw close to God. With-
bur - den me As they laugh and mock. All
falls re - sound Mak - ing moun - tains shake! Deep
com - fort give Through your dark - est night; Yet

in my heart are flam - ing fires For the Lord on high.
night from tears I am not free; Would that I could die!
wa - ters surg - ing all a - round O - ver-whelm my soul.
while I live I long for God, For the liv - ing Lord.

120   O Give Thanks to the Lord

°MIHAMEK

Psalm 136:1-18, 21-26 (Grail)

Amis song, Taiwan
Transcr. and adapt. by I-TO LOH, 1981

1. O give thanks to the Lord for he is good,
2. Who a - lone has wrought mar - vel - ous works,
3. It was he who made the great lights,
4. The first - born of the E - gyp - tians he smote,
5. He di - vid - ed the Red Sea in two,
6. Through the des - ert his peo - ple he led,
7. He let Is - rael in - her - it their land,
8. And he snatch'd us a - way from our foes,

For God's stead - fast love en - dures for - ev - er.

For God's love en - dures for - ev - er.

For God's love en - dures for - ev - er.

1. Give thanks to the God of gods.
2. Whose wis - dom it was made the skies,
3. The sun to rule in the day,
4. He brought Is - rael out from their midst,
5. He made Is - rael pass through the midst,
6. Na - tions in their great - ness he struck,
7. On his ser - vants their land he be - stowed,
8. He gives food to all liv - ing things,

For God's stead - fast love en - dures for - ev - er.

For God's love en - dures for - ev - er.

For God's love en - dures for - ev - er.

Transcr. and adapt. copyright © 1983 by I-to Loh.

Psalm 136, from *The Psalms: A New Translation* published by William Collins Sons & Co. Ltd., is reprinted by permission of the Grail, England.

PSALMS

Taiwanese

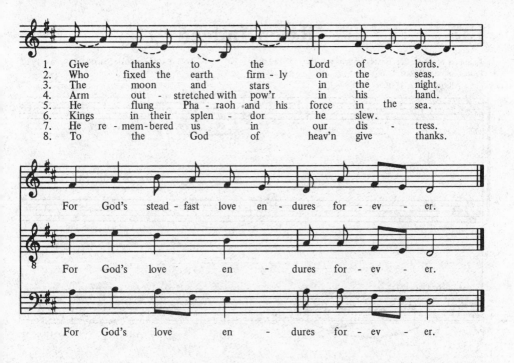

1. Give thanks to the Lord of lords.
2. Who fixed the earth firm - ly on the seas.
3. The moon and stars in the night.
4. Arm out - stretched with pow'r in his hand.
5. He flung Pha - raoh and his force in the sea.
6. Kings in their splen - dor he slew.
7. He re - mem - bered us in our dis - tress.
8. To the God of heav'n give thanks.

For God's stead - fast love en - dures for - ev - er.

For God's love en - dures for - ev - er.

For God's love en - dures for - ev - er.

Let All Nations Praise the Lord 121

°KATIPOL

Psalm 117 (TEV, alt.)

Puyama Song, Taiwan
Transcr. and adapt. by I-TO LOH, 1981

Unison (♩ = 108 or faster)

Let all na - tions, let all na - tions, come, praise the Lord.

All peo - ples, praise him, praise him, his love for us is strong. Praise him,

all peo - ples, praise him, and his faith - ful - ness is e - ter - nal.

Taiwanese

122   °Risen Indeed

Antiphon of praise for Easter or general use
PAUL LINCOLN SMITH

PAUL LINCOLN SMITH, 1969, rev. 1980

Allegro (♩ = c. 100)

Praise!

Praise!

Cantor (freely)

Praise!   All   peo - ple

All   peo - ple   praise!   O praise the

praise!   Praise the Lord!

Words and music copyright © 1969, 1983 by Paul Lincoln Smith.

Performance suggestion: A capella is preferred, but the chorus part may by doubled by the organ or piano. The asterisks indicate optional ornaments by skilled soloist.

Luke 24:34

123

Psalm 23

MU-JEN

Psalm 23
Para. by ESTHER RICE, 1981

Chinese traditional melody
Attr. to Mr. FU

(♩ = c. 84)

1. O Je - ho - vah my Lord, my shep - herd are you.
2. Though I walk through the vale shad - owed by dark death,
3. All my life, O my God, yes, all my life long,

You are at my side; nev - er shall I want. You make me lie down
I will fear no ill, for I know that you Will be with me still;
Love and mer - cy shall sure - ly fol - low me. Yes, all my life long,

in the pas - tures green; By the wa - ters still you are lead - ing me.
yes, your rod and staff Give to me as - sur - ance of peace and rest.
all my length of days Shall your love and mer - cy still fol - low me.

You re - new my soul, give to my spir - it life. For your own name's sake
Here be - fore my foes have you pre - pared a feast. You have a - noint - ed
Yes, your love and mer - cy fol - low af - ter me. Sure - ly Je - ho - vah's

you lead in right path - ways. For your own name's sake,
me with oil of glad - ness So that my cup is
house shall be my dwell - ing. Sure - ly Je - ho - vah's

you lead in right path - ways. Yes, in righ - teous path ways.
full to o - ver - flow - ing, Full to o - ver - flow - ing.
house shall be my dwell - ing, Al - ways and for - ev - er.

Para. copyright © 1983 by Esther Rice.

Sing a Song to the Lord

SALIDUMMAY

Based on Psalm 96
FRANCISCO F. FELICIANO

BEN PANGOSBAN, 1980

Very lively (♩ = c. 120)

1. Sing a song, sing a song to the Lord,
2. Great is God, wor - thy of all praise,
3. Tribes on earth, bow, con - fess God's might,
4. Tell the na - tions God reigns as King,

All the world, sing and bless the Name,
Wor - ship God high a - bove all things,
Bow down and give all glo - ry due,
Judg - ing with truth and righ - teous - ness,

Ay, ay, sa - li - dum - may,* Ay ay, sa - li - dum - may.

Dai - ly sing of the sav - ing power, Tell all
Who with might made the u - ni - verse, Hon - or
Come to God, bring your gifts most rare; fill heav'n's
Sing a song, sing a song to the Lord, All the

lands of the won - drous works; Ay, ay, sa - li - dum -
give to God's maj - es - ty,
hall with your joy - ful sound.
world sing and bless God's name,

may, Ay, ay sal - li - dum - may.

Music copyright © 1983 by Ben Pangosban.
Words copyright © 1983 by Francisco F. Feliciano.
Used by permission of the Christian Conference of Asia.
*"Salidummay" means "sing joyously"

Performance suggestion: A continuously interlocking pattern $\frac{2}{4}$ *played on bamboo buzzers can provide a*

rhythmical accompaniment. +*and* ○*indicate closing and opening the hole of the buzzers respectively.*

Filipino

PSALMS

125 The Lord Is My Shepherd

°DALINDAY

Psalm 23 (RSV)

Melody based on Manobo Dalinday
PRISCILLA MAGDAMO, 1981

The Lord is my Shepherd, I shall not want;
He makes me lie down in green pastures. He leads me beside still wa - ters; He re-

stores my soul. He leads me in the paths of righ - teous - ness for his name's sake.

Even though I walk through I fear no evil; Your rod and your staff,
the valley of the shadow of death, for you are with me;

Music copyright © 1983 by Priscilla Magdamo.
Text (alt.) from the Revised Standard Version Common Bible, copyrighted © 1973.

Indexes

127 INDEX OF COMPOSERS/ARRANGERS, AUTHORS/TRANSLATORS, AND SOURCES

128

III. TOPICAL INDEX

GOD
Creation of God: 2, 3, 4, 5, 8, 9, 16, 17, 19, 21, 27, 31, 54, 71, 91, 92, 103, 120
Gifts of God: 2, 4, 5, 6, 7, 9, 10, 12, 14, 16, 17, 18, 20, 26, 43, 57, 65, 71, 89, 103, 120
Glory of God: 4, 5, 12, 17, 25, 44, 46, 90, 124
Grace of God: 3, 4, 9, 14, 21, 22, 45, 63, 78, 84, 87, 97, 109, 112, 115, 117, 118, 120
Kingdom of God: 48, 60, 63, 68, 69, 74, 85, 95, 98, 106, 112
Love of God: 8, 9, 12, 13, 15, 20, 45, 48, 53, 63, 79, 84, 91, 92, 94, 96, 102, 103, 114, 115, 119, 120, 121
Presence of God: 19, 20, 25, 30, 58, 61, 77, 109, 113, 114, 119
Word of God: 23, 38, 41, 49, 50, 65, 78, 92, 106

RESPONSES TO GOD
Commitment: 27, 39, 40, 42, 54, 62, 64, 71, 79, 82, 87, 92, 93, 107, 108
Doxologies, Amens, Blessings: 15, 104, 118
Hallelujahs: 10, 28, 32, 122
Praise and Worship: 3, 5, 6, 7, 8, 9, 10, 11, 12, 15, 16, 17, 18, 19, 21, 25, 31, 39, 41, 43, 44, 45, 60, 67, 77, 81, 89, 91, 96, 99, 102, 104, 106, 113, 114, 120, 121, 124
Prayer: 2, 6, 13, 14, 24, 26, 36, 37, 44, 49, 63, 70, 73, 80, 84, 88, 95, 97, 111, 113, 115
Thanksgivings: 3, 9, 16, 17, 21, 26, 27, 31, 36, 44, 45, 65, 67, 80, 81, 89, 91, 111, 115, 120

JESUS CHRIST
Adoration: 10, 11, 34, 104, 111
Advent, Christmas, Incarnation: 1, 23, 29, 30, 33, 34, 40, 42, 43, 46, 51, 52, 62, 92, 99, 102
Easter—Resurrection: 4, 28, 32, 39, 107, 122
Epiphany, Witness, Proclamation: 47, 75, 78, 95, 102
Life and Presence: 10, 12, 37, 56, 75, 95, 97, 98, 101, 111
Passion and Crucifixion: 50, 53, 79, 82

JESUS CHRIST *(continued)*
Victory of Christ: 1, 11, 28, 32, 39, 57, 85

THE CHRISTIAN LIFE
Affirmation and Truth: 2, 37, 38, 57, 64, 82, 85, 101, 105, 106, 110, 116, 124
Aspiration and Hope: 24, 45, 53, 54, 59, 62, 63, 67, 72, 106, 107, 108, 119
Comfort and Healing: 2, 14, 20, 49, 52, 53, 54, 58, 61, 64, 69, 73, 75, 83, 89, 94, 95, 108, 110, 111, 115, 117, 119, 123, 125
Confession, Mercy, Forgiveness: 6, 44, 55, 56, 58, 64, 67, 74, 76, 80, 85, 97, 116
Discipleship, Service, and Mission: 27, 35, 45, 54, 57, 59, 60, 62, 64, 65, 67, 70, 71, 74, 75, 77, 78, 79, 80, 82, 83, 84, 85, 86, 87, 88, 96, 107, 108
Faith and Trust: 2, 7, 13, 41, 53, 56, 69, 73, 79, 83, 96, 98, 106, 108, 109, 110, 113, 117, 123, 125
Guidance: 14, 20, 21, 24, 37, 38, 42, 44, 47, 49, 52, 54, 58, 59, 61, 62, 69, 74, 79, 90, 94, 96, 97, 105, 107, 109, 110, 112, 123, 125
Liberation and Justice: 24, 54, 59, 67, 72, 75, 76, 82, 84, 85, 95, 112
Life, Death, and Parting: 28, 53, 61, 77, 82, 83, 105, 107, 123, 125
Love and Grace: 2, 6, 11, 12, 17, 21, 26, 31, 35, 37, 41, 48, 49, 53, 59, 63, 66, 68, 87, 105, 109, 112, 118, 123, 125
Peace and Joy: 6, 10, 11, 19, 26, 31, 41, 48, 58, 68, 74, 78, 80, 87, 89, 105, 112, 118
Renewal: 14, 85, 90
Salvation: 1, 23, 28, 32, 39, 40, 48, 52, 57, 64, 66, 67, 68, 73, 76, 77, 78, 79, 85, 91, 102, 111, 116, 124

THE HOLY SPIRIT AND THE CHURCH
The Holy Spirit: 13, 14, 24, 73, 104
The Church: 31, 36, 47, 96, 106
Care for the Community: 26, 47, 60, 62, 66, 67, 75, 86, 89, 112

THE HOLY SPIRIT AND THE CHURCH *(cont.)*
Unity and Fellowship: 27, 32, 35, 37, 45, 47, 48, 54, 59, 71, 76, 78, 112
Holy Communion: 30, 36
The Lord's Day: 6

LIGHT AND DARKNESS
Light and Darkness: 3, 23, 52, 63, 68, 73, 74, 82, 89, 90

PEOPLE OF FAITH
The Saints: 21, 36, 82

PEOPLE OF FAITH *(continued)*
The Family: 26, 70, 87, 92, 93
Biblical Figures: 22, 55, 56, 94

USEFUL MUSICAL TYPES
Call and Response: 10, 11, 15, 28, 40, 104, 116, 120, 122
Rounds, Canons: 99, 115, 121
Solos: 19, 30, 50, 51, 55, 66, 110, 111, 125
Unaccompanied: 8, 10, 11, 14, 17, 18, 34, 40, 43, 76, 113, 114, 116, 118, 121, 123
Descants: 64, 118
Instrumental Parts: 19, 20, 29, 32, 59, 75, 124

129   IV. INDEX OF BIBLICAL REFERENCES

130

V. INDEX OF TUNE NAMES

INDEX OF TUNE NAMES